T0277939

OLD TRUTHS AND NEW CLICHÉS

Old Truths
and
New Cliches

ESSAYS BY

ISAAC BASHEVIS SINGER

Edited by DAVID STROMBERG

PRINCETON UNIVERSITY PRESS

PRINCETON AND OXFORD

Published by Princeton University Press
41 William Street, Princeton, New Jersey 08540
99 Banbury Road, Oxford OX2 6JX

press.princeton.edu

Library of Congress Cataloging-in-Publication Data

Names: Singer, Isaac Bashevis, 1903–1991, author. | Stromberg, David, 1980– editor.
Title: Old truths and new clichés / essays by Isaac Bashevis Singer ;
    edited by David Stromberg.
Description: Princeton : Princeton University Press, [2022] | Includes bibliographical references and index.
Identifiers: LCCN 2021033990 | ISBN 9780691217635 (hardback ; acid-free paper)
Subjects: LCSH: Singer, Isaac Bashevis, 1903–1991—Translations into English. |
    LCGFT: Essays.
Classification: LCC PJ5129.S49 O43 2022 | DDC 839/.143—dc23
LC record available at https://lccn.loc.gov/2021033990

British Library Cataloging-in-Publication Data is available

Editorial: Anne Savarese and James Collier
Production Editorial: Ellen Foos
Text Design: Karl Spurzem
Jacket/Cover Design: Pamela L.Schnitter
Production: Erin Suydam
Publicity: Kate Hensley and Carmen Hensley
Copyeditor: Jodi Beder

Jacket image: Isaac Bashevis Singer, 1978. © Yousuf Karsh

This book has been composed in Arno Pro

Printed on acid-free paper. ∞

Printed in the United States of America

10 9 8 7 6 5 4 3 2 1

To the blessed memory of Israel Zamir (1929–2014)

CONTENTS

PERSONAL WRITINGS AND PHILOSOPHY

This volume offers a representative collection of Isaac Bashevis Singer's essays on those topics and themes that characterized his literary career. It is neither a definitive edition of his essayistic writing nor a facsimile of archival materials. Instead this collection brings together essays selected for translation into English by Singer himself. And while it does not replace archival research, the volume gives readers insight into the different stages of Singer's creative process and intellectual development.

Many of these essays were presented as lectures. In a few cases, the published Yiddish originals show that Singer intended, during the composition, to read the essay aloud to a live audience—though the piece was printed in a newspaper, the text directly addresses a group of listeners who are not there. This means that Singer was consciously composing in Yiddish a text that he knew had a target audience who understood only English—and that its Yiddish publication was only one step in its final form. Singer was also involved in every stage of their translation, either translating himself orally while a collaborator typed up his sentences, or correcting translations made by others.

It is possible, then, to read these texts not quite as translations, but as original works produced through a process that included a first draft in Yiddish, translation into English, and English-language revisions made by Singer alone—sometimes undergoing two, three, or more drafts, with corrections or additions that do not appear in the original Yiddish texts. The final piece in the collection—a rhymed poem written and corrected in the original English—reveals Singer's own compositional tendencies in his second language. In this sense, this book is more than a collection of Singer's translated articles. It is a cohesive work, expressed in Singer's own voice.

Singer was a modular thinker. The topics and themes of his essays can be generally separated into the three categories making up the parts of this collection—the literary arts, Yiddish and Jewish life, and personal writings and philosophy—with each mode incorporating aspects of the others. Yet Singer's thinking was modular *within* each category too, so that over his long career— spanning more than sixty years—he often developed, expanded, and shifted intuitions or convictions he had held from the very beginning. With this in mind, the pieces in this volume are those that reflect the most expanded and nuanced take on their topic. They are included because they express a central element of Singer's intellectual foundation—a testament to the spirit of his artistic vision.

—*David Stromberg, Jerusalem*

Writers Don't Write for the Drawer

AN INTRODUCTION TO THE
ESSAYS OF ISAAC BASHEVIS SINGER

Isaac Bashevis Singer has long been acknowledged as a master storyteller. But his critical writings have been largely passed over. One underlying reason is the sheer volume of Singer's output. Starting in 1939, when he became a regular contributor to the Yiddish daily *Forverts*, he produced an incredible amount of text. He published his work under at least three pseudonyms, any number of which might appear in a single issue—sometimes on a single page—in a variety of genres: stories, novels, memoirs, essays, literary sketches, satires, dialogues, travel pieces, reviews, and even a popular media digest.

In the early 1960s, as his popularity grew, Singer's Yiddish-language production was increasingly accompanied by efforts to translate, edit, and adapt his work for English-speaking audiences. By then, he had accumulated untranslated material from nearly forty years of writing, and was still producing new material, including some of the works for which he would be best known. He also began to appear as a lecturer, traveling to universities, synagogues, community centers, and retreats all across the United States, giving talks on everything from literature, to Kabbalah, to his own concept of religion. It was, as Singer told *Harper's* in 1965, "a lot of work for a man of sixty." Indeed, it seemed the literary and intellectual factory that became Isaac Bashevis Singer never stopped for breath.

Yet the amount that a given person can write is always limited—and not only by the number of days they are destined to live on the planet. Singer's creative process, which came to include a practice of writing, translating, and editing, was limited by how much English-language text he could prepare—especially since he often did the translations himself with a collaborator, or, less often, supervised and corrected translations made by others. He was also limited by the number of books his publisher could consider, print, advertise, and distribute at any given moment—in part because of the risk of saturating the market with his works. All these issues may seem superfluous where the noble issues of art and literature are concerned. But they are quite relevant in considering Singer, whose full career as a writer is traced only when taking into account all of his publications in the Yiddish press, and whose book publications—whether in Yiddish or in English, the two languages in which he worked with equal authority—reveal only a partial view of his artistic output.

This partialness becomes especially clear when considering Singer's essays. The way that these essays were written, translated, edited, and, in some cases, presented to audiences, reflects the central role they played in Singer's literary life. Many of them first appeared under the pseudonym Yitskhok Varshavski—Isaac from Warsaw, which Yiddish readers could have recognized as Yitskhok Bashevis, since he openly cited the real titles of his best-known works—and some under his other pseudonym, D. Segal. Yet after being translated, edited, and rewritten in English, they all appeared under the name Isaac Bashevis Singer. The final manuscripts left behind, as well as drafts used to prepare them, provide some of the clearest views into

Singer as a literary artist—one who is able not only to produce fiction that captivated readers, but also to discuss the aesthetic, spiritual, and moral vision undergirding all of his writing. The essays also reflect the ideas that drove his literary production. In this, they are an embodiment of his accomplishment twice over.

Singer was a writer. But he was also an intellectual. You can hear this in voice recordings, less so in English than in Yiddish, where all traces of sentimentality and schtick fall away. In Yiddish, Singer doesn't have a Yiddish accent. He doesn't sound like someone's grandfather—or great-grandfather—as he sometimes does in English. He sounds like a writer whose mind is constantly working and whose critical eye penetrates beyond everyday illusions into what drives human nature, no less than to what lifts the human spirit. The closest Singer got to leaving a record of this voice in English was when he presented ideas about art and literature, Yiddish and Jewish culture, and his personal experience and philosophy—all of which are at the center of these essays.

Bringing this material together requires a particular kind of attention. The fact that many of these works were not prepared for final publication by their author means that a myriad of editorial decisions have to be made along the way. This is especially true when, looking for the Yiddish material used to prepare the English-language essays, we see that Singer sometimes translated, edited, and incorporated materials from a number of articles, some of them published years apart. Many of these essays synthesize years of reflection on various topics and considerable editing and revising during the translation, creating final versions in English that no longer reflect any existing Yiddish original. Later, as Singer becomes more practiced, he brings this synthesis directly into the original versions, so that, at some point, some essays *do* appear as direct translations of the Yiddish. In yet other cases, none of the original Yiddish material has been found, so that all we have are several corrected English-language drafts.

The challenge for an editor collecting these essays is to treat each work on its own terms, to take into account its specific provenance, and yet to give the volume coherence as a whole—all this while adhering to the author's own articulated artistic vision. As such, this collection is itself a *synthetic* work, in that it aims to bring together essays published or presented in a variety of venues, but also to create a single, cohesive volume. Since this editorial effort is itself grounded in both historical and literary concerns, it seems prudent to set out two of the central circumstances that have guided this work: first, Singer's own aborted efforts to publish a collection of essays, and second, the complex translation and editing process that some of these essays underwent.

Singer's earliest English-language publication in the United States, an epic historical novel titled *The Family Moskat* (1950) and published by Alfred A. Knopf, was a misadventure in translation, editing, and marketing that ended with the publisher's losing interest in his future works.* Singer's next publisher, Noonday, was founded by Cecil Hemley—a writer, editor, and translator whose wife, Elaine Gottlieb, also translated Singer's work. Noonday published three of his books—*Satan in Goray* (1955), *Gimpel the Fool and Other Stories* (1957), and *The Magician of Lublin* (1960)—before being acquired by Farrar, Straus and Giroux (FSG), which published *The Spinoza of Market Street and Other*

---

* Singer's translator, A. H. Gross, died before completing the translation, and Singer undertook the rest of the work with Gross's daughter, Nancy Gross, as well as Maurice Samuel and Lyon Mearson. For a history of Singer's experiences with Knopf, see Paul Kresh, *Isaac Bashevis Singer, the Magician of West 86th Street: A Biography* (New York: Dial Press, 1979), 184, and the Knopf papers at the Harry Ransom Papers Center, including the increasingly acrimonious relationship between Singer and his editor.

Stories (1961) and *The Slave* (1962). By 1963, FSG had acquired Singer's second large historical epic, published in English in two parts as *The Manor* and *The Estate*, which Gottlieb was then translating. In June, a memo from Roger Straus to Robert Giroux and others described what Straus called the "Singer editorial story." With this major translation effort in the works, FSG was planning a three-book deal: a first-person novel, likely *A Ship to America*, which Singer was publishing that year in Yiddish; a memoir collection, which later appeared as *In My Father's Court*; and an untitled collection of essays. Straus describes the collection as pulling from "a wealth of essays, nonfiction, prepared over the past thirty years and never translated, but from which Isaac Singer will someday wish to select a volume. These essays are on philosophy, literature, and include some lectures." In August 1963, Singer again mentions this idea in his own letter to Straus, but appears to hedge against the possibility. "I would like to call your attention," Singer writes, "to the fact that a collection of essays is still a remote possibility, since very few of them were translated until now." The next year instead saw Singer's third collection, *Short Friday and Other Stories* (1964), while all discussion of either the first-person novel or the essay collection ended.

In his letter, Straus had referred to Singer's essays written over the previous thirty years, suggesting that, regardless of the possibilities discussed, Singer considered including his two Warsaw-era essays—"Verter oder bilder" (Words or Images) and "Tsu der frage vegn dikhtung un politik" (Toward the Question of Poetics and Politics)—written well before his 1935 arrival in New York.* At this point, it seems, both Singer and his publishers

---

* Singer, "Verter oder bilder" (Words or Images), *Literarishe Bleter*, August 26, 1927, 663–65; "Tsu der frage vegn dikhtung un politik" (Toward the Question of Poetics and Politics), *Globus* 1, no. 3 (Sept. 1932): 39–49.

considered building his career according to the European intellectual tradition, as an author who produced both literary and philosophical writings.* But it seems that, as his understanding of the cultural landscape around him grew, Singer changed course, building his path to critical recognition through the role of an old fashioned storyteller with a devilish streak. His commercial success coincided with his shedding of the intellectual aspect of his public persona, and his cultivation of a new image, that of a translated old-world transplant. In reality, he was a modern writer, well versed in the various streams of world literature, and working between two languages—composing and publishing first in Yiddish, and translating himself into English with the help of collaborators and editors.

The years between the early 1960s and the mid-1980s saw an increasingly hectic schedule of writing and translating—especially upon the publication of *Zlateh the Goat* (1966), his first collection for children, after which he produced seventeen more children's books—and more traveling for lectures. Singer's personal philosophy was funneled into stories, interviews, and, after receiving the 1978 Nobel Prize for Literature, a book titled *Conversations with Isaac Bashevis Singer* (1985), coauthored with Richard Burgin, who recorded and organized Singer's ideas. The next mention of Singer's essays appears in a proposal, submitted by his secretary Dvorah Menashe Telushkin in the fall of 1986, to collect his untranslated essays. The proposal re-

---

* For detailed histories of Singer's years as a writer in Warsaw, as well as his first two years in America, see David Stromberg, "'Your Papers for a Tourist Visa': A Literary-Biographical Consideration of Isaac Bashevis Singer in Warsaw, 1923–1935," in *The European Journal of Jewish Studies* 15.2 (2021): 256–84; and "'Don't Be Hopeless, Kid': A Literary-Biographical Consideration of Isaac Bashevis Singer's First Years in New York, 1935–1937," *Studies in American Jewish Literature* 40.2 (2021): 109–39.

fers to "over . . . 800 essays" that appeared "under three pseudonyms . . . in Yiddish newspapers in Poland and in the United
States," and concludes that "the only reason these works have
not been previously translated is that they had been forgotten,
and relegated to the archives of a few libraries and Yiddish research organizations."* Roger Straus appears to refer to this
proposal in a letter to Singer dated July 1987, saying he would
speak to Singer when they next met about a book called *First
Steps in Literature*, which appears to correspond to the first volume of the proposal. There is also a mention, in an unsigned
handwritten memo from July 1987, of a manuscript titled *Broken
Tablets*, possibly referring to the third volume, which is also
mentioned in a memo from May 1988 describing it as an
English-language "collection of nonfiction and articles." None
of these efforts appears to have ever materialized—very likely
because both Telushkin's proposal and Straus's letter are dated
from around the time that Singer began to suffer the onset of
dementia.

   Israel Zamir, Singer's only child, records in his memoir of his
father that, in 1986, "the last year his mind was still clear," Singer
"was still making abundant plans" that included writing "a popular children's book about the chronicles of philosophy throughout the world."† Lester Goran, Singer's last literary collaborator,
recalls in his own memoir about working with the aging Yiddish
author that this period was especially difficult. He mentions

---

   * Telushkin proposes a three-volume collection, selected with Professor Chone
Shmeruk of the Hebrew University, the first volume titled *Early Stories, 1924–49*, the
second titled *From the Old and New Home*, a memoir published by Singer in the
Forverts in 1963–65 as *Fun der alter un nayer heym*, and the third titled *Literary Meet-
ings, Essays, and Critiques, 1939–1949*.
   † Israel Zamir, *Journey to My Father: Isaac Bashevis Singer*, trans. Barbara Harshav
(New York: Arcade Publishing, 1995), 231.

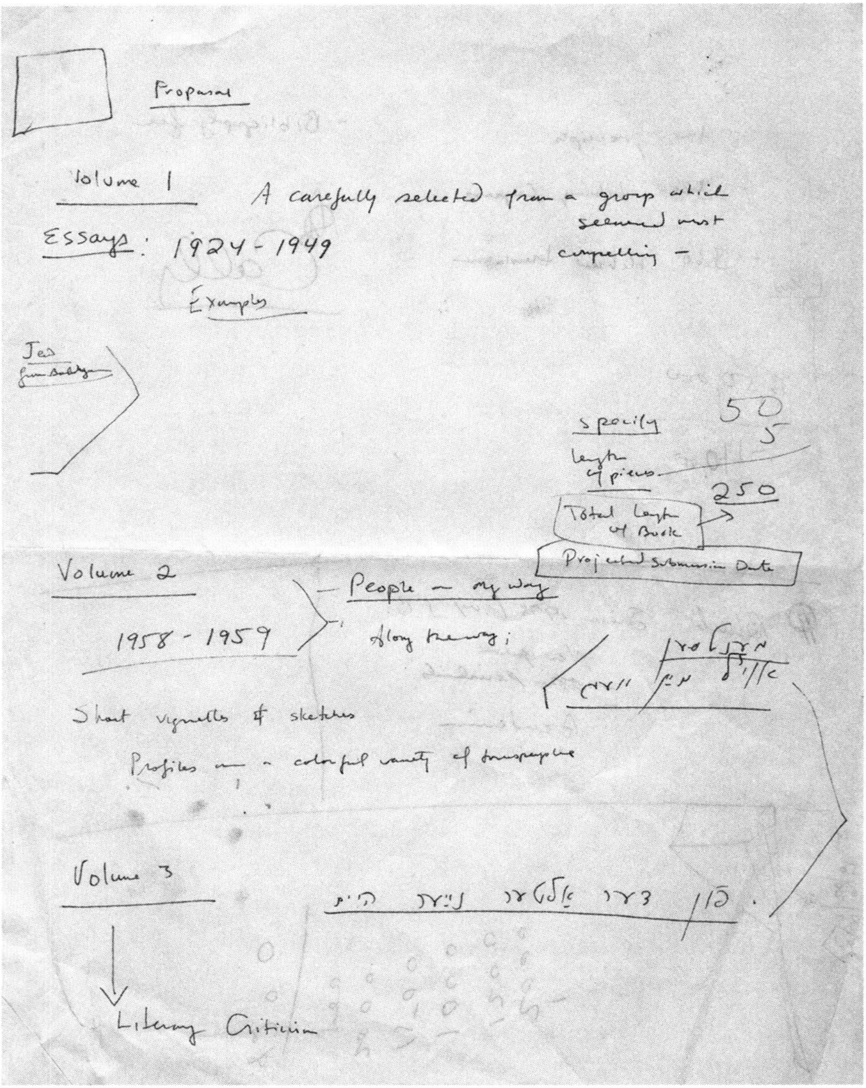

FIGURE 1. A draft proposal for a three-volume collection of Singer's nonfiction in Dvorah Menashe Telushkin's handwriting. Dvorah Telushkin Collection of Isaac Bashevis Singer Papers, Harry Ransom Center, University of Texas at Austin.

Singer's fantasies about their writing a "master work" that would make them both wealthy. "Singer told me one morning the time had come for the two of us to finally write a great book together," writes Goran. "The book was to probe the depths of what he truly believed. . . . His genuine philosophies would be revealed. . . . It would be a work that would change people's minds about him."* Singer was serious enough about this work, Goran reports, to involve the former regional manager of Doubleday, Gordon Weel, in trying to sell the proposed book to publishers, some of which expressed interest. The book even acquired a working title: *God's Fugitives*. In April 1987, over breakfast, Singer told to Goran they would start writing the book that instant. Intending to hand him a pencil, Singer instead handed him a fork. When Goran pointed this out, Singer said he was losing his mind, and handed Goran another pencil—this time in the form of a butter knife. When Goran finally procured a pencil from a waitress, Singer began to tell him the same life story he had told countless times. As Goran writes, "*God's Fugitives* was the last gasp of the impossible."† And Singer's final plans for a nonfiction collection dissipated yet again.

While he was alive, Singer's American career was dominated by both literary principles and publishing pragmatics. When opportunities presented themselves, he pursued them, prioritizing those that were most realizable. In rare cases did he insist on publishing a work that was deemed unmarketable by his literary consultants, as was the case with *The Penitent* (1983), the translation of which was completed ten years before it was published—and which only appeared once Singer had secured

* Lester Goran, *The Bright Streets of Surfside: The Memoir of a Friendship with Isaac Bashevis Singer* (Kent, OH: Kent State University Press, 1994), 139.
† Goran, *The Bright Streets of Surfside*, 152.

the Nobel Prize.* But his vision for a literary career did not always overlap with his publisher's plans. In some cases, he invested time and money in translating his works, only to have his agent or publisher suggest setting the manuscript aside.

This did not slow Singer down: between 1955 and 1988, he published ten novels, eleven short story collections, and four autobiographical works, as well as eighteen books for children. But his public activity revealed only part of the work that he was producing in English. In his archive lie numerous novels, stories, and memoirs, many of them corrected in his own hand, all of which he deemed publishable, but which were set aside for practical reasons. And among those carefully wrought materials, a mini-corpus of essays is revealed: a collection of material implicitly prepared by Singer, piece by piece, through his choice for which works to translate. These essays, along with other unpublished work, accumulated in Singer's "chaos room"—the walk-in closet where he kept manuscripts, clippings, notebooks, certificates, diplomas, awards, letters, and many other documents and objects connected with his literary and personal life.

Singer knew his work would be left undone when he passed away. His son recalls, during the last visit when his mind was clear, Singer going into the chaos room and saying, "Oh, my God, I've got to live another hundred years to edit the stories, translate them into English, and publish them"—and he did produce enough material to translate, edit, and publish books for several more decades.† In 1993, two years after his death,

---

* For a discussion of this novel's publication history in Yiddish and English, see David Stromberg, *Narrative Faith: Dostoevsky, Camus, and Singer* (Newark: University of Delaware Press, 2018).

† Zamir, *Journey to My Father*, 231–32.

these materials were all acquired by the Harry Ransom Center, and the essays were sent, along with everything in the chaos room, to Austin, Texas, where they were catalogued with the help of the late Yiddish scholar Joseph Sherman. I arrived at Singer's archive on the trail of on an unpublished Yiddish booklet titled "Rebellion and Prayer, or The True Protester," which he says in *The New York Times* was written during the Holocaust.* Sitting in Jerusalem and scouring the online finding aid, I discovered that the most similarly titled entry, "To the True Protester," was an English-language poem—written on the back of a letter from his German publisher dated August 13, 1980—which now closes this collection. I eventually made it to the archive itself, and there, scattered among his papers, found his translated but uncollected essays. Straus had written, in his 1963 memo, that Singer would "someday wish to select a volume" of essays from his critical writings. His choice of which works to translate reflects this selection.

Singer's essays found their main audience on the lecture circuit. And while he solicited translators and collaborators—paid and unpaid, credited and uncredited—to help render first drafts in English, he did all of the editing and revising himself. Singer was a seasoned translator, having brought authors such as Thomas Mann, Knut Hamsun, and Erich Maria Remarque into Yiddish. And though he never openly admitted to translating himself into English, he addressed the issue at a 1964 lecture on literary

---

* Richard Burgin and Isaac Bashevis Singer, *Conversations with Isaac Bashevis Singer*, p. 52. For a discussion of Singer's reference to this essay in his author's note to *The Penitent*, where he also engages in a philosophical dialogue with his character's stated positions, see David Stromberg, "Rebellion and Creativity: Contextualizing Isaac Bashevis Singer's 'Author's Note' to *The Penitent*," *In geveb*, June 2016.

method. In response to a question about translation, he re-
sponds, "I used to have translators, but now I do a lot of the
translation myself. I translate word by word, and I have a collaborator who helps me organize the sentences so that they
should sound more English. Because in my case I know the
words, but I don't know the construction of the English sentence so well as a man who was born here."* Still, even this
admission is partial because, as the draft essays demonstrate,
his literary efforts involved much more than translation. Singer's authorial hand is evident on the typescripts, not only in
the ideas expressed, but also in the editorial cuts and corrections he made. Once he had working drafts, he took out his pen
and, in his own hand, began to pick the essays apart—cutting,
rewriting, and sometimes restructuring them directly in
English.

Like much of Singer's writing, his long-form essays appeared
as installments, each marked as a continuation of an earlier one.
But, unlike his fiction or memoir work, the installments sometimes appeared weeks apart, and the essays lacked the plot element to ground their content from one installment to the next.
This made it challenging for readers, especially anyone who did
not follow the *Forverts* regularly, to connect the pieces and understand their conceptual breadth or scope. Published as they
were, these pieces were perceived—by both general readers and
Yiddish critics—as throwaways used to fill up a weekly quota
of text. Even those who followed Singer's work closely, including Yiddish scholars, tended to consider anything not published

---

* Singer, lecture on literary method, January 29, 1964 (sound recording, 7″ sound
reel, Harry Ransom Center, University of Texas at Austin).

under the Bashevis pseudonym to have lesser literary quality.* And as David Neal Miller has suggested, Yiddish scholars are often tempted "to regard Segal as a less conscientious Varshavski, much as Singer has characterized Varshavski as a less conscientious Bashevis"—not least because Singer perpetuated these distinctions.† But what Miller says of Segal holds for Varshavski as well: "the opposite is true."‡ Singer deployed these pseudonyms strategically: they allowed him to treat a variety of topics under different guises, and, perhaps more importantly, to publish prolifically without having his name appear all over the paper. Most importantly—and this relates to his essays no less than to his works of fiction and memoir—Singer had recourse to all the Yiddish writing that he produced under each of these names as potential material for translating, editing, and rewriting in English, always publishing this material as Isaac Bashevis Singer.

Singer rarely produced material he did not intend to publish. Indeed, the second installment of "Who Needs Literature?" was originally titled "Writers Don't Write 'for the Drawer'"—a conviction he bore out to the end of his life. Singer did not write for the drawer, and the fact that his essayistic work was an important facet of his oeuvre is further evinced by his placement of some of these works, from the early 1960s until almost the end of his life, in a variety of newspapers, journals, magazines,

---

* This tendency has extended into criticism of Singer's work in later decades, as, for example, when Jan Schwarz writes that "Singer's best work was published under the name Yitskhok Bashevis in Yiddish journals and newspapers" (*Survivors and Exiles: Yiddish Culture after the Holocaust.* [Detroit: Wayne State University Press, 2015], 231).

† David Neal Miller, *Fear of Fiction: Narrative Strategies in the Works of Isaac Bashevis Singer* (Albany: SUNY Press, 1985), 58.

‡ Ibid.

pamphlets, and anthologies. And though, during his lifetime, he constantly gave interviews in which he summarized many of his ideas, no source expresses them as directly as his essays.* That he did not have the chance to collect them into a single volume means only that the work was left for others to complete.

In many cases, the Yiddish publication history of these essays, appearing in the *Forverts* under various pseudonyms, undermined their significance within Singer's corpus. The only essays to receive critical attention during his lifetime were those published in Yiddish literary journals, but they were no more or less central to his development as an author—or to the theoretical framework driving his literary production—than what appeared in the newspaper. Singer's emphasis on translating his own writing, for example, was grounded in the concepts and methods of a modern author working in the context of world literature. Yet members of the Yiddish literary community rarely acknowledged the deliberateness of these efforts. This left many of them ambivalent about his position as the unofficial spokesperson of Yiddish literature in America—a circumstance so prominent it was parodied by Cynthia Ozick in "Envy; or, Yiddish in America" (1969).† In addition, with his English-language publications focused on fiction, he and his publisher continued to cultivate his image as an old fashioned storyteller rather than a modernist writer with intellectual leanings like Albert Camus or Vladimir Nabokov, promoting his persona as a worldly sage. Finally, while

---

* For a collection of Singer's interviews, see Isaac Bashevis Singer, *Conversations* (1992).

† For discussions of Ozick's story, and its place in American literary history, see Leah Garrett, "Cynthia Ozick's 'Envy': A Reconsideration," *Studies in American Jewish Literature* 24 (2005): 60–81 and Kathryn Hellerstein, "The Envy of Yiddish: Cynthia Ozick as Translator," *Studies in American Jewish Literature* 31, no. 1 (2012): 24–47.

several critics working in American literary studies discussed the philosophical themes driving his work in the early 1960s, most had no access to Yiddish, leaving his critical ideas beyond the scope of material they could consider in their research.* The scholarly trajectory set out in the 1960s has stuck for decades—and, to this day, few critics deal seriously with Singer's essayistic writings.

Despite his authorial persona being increasingly bound to his image as a storyteller, and the prospects of releasing an essay collection being repeatedly put off for the sake of more fiction, Singer never abandoned his intellectual pursuits. After receiving the 1978 Nobel Prize in Literature, he gained new authority as a writer on the world stage and was invited to lecture with increasing frequency. In this context, he returned to a number of his core essays, many of which were written in the 1960s, translating and revising them for new audiences. In the spring of 1979, for example, he was invited by the Gallatin Division of New York University to speak in a lecture series titled "The Writer at Work," and turned to an essay on the nature of divinity and religion first published in 1966—a moving reflection on the nature of faith in modern times titled "A Personal Concept of Religion"—which he now translated and rewrote in English. Two versions of the essay appeared in English in Singer's lifetime, the first in excerpts from the NYU lecture in *The New York Times* under the title "What Is God to Do—Discuss His Book with Every Reader?" and the second as a pamphlet, published by the University of Southern Louisiana as the 1980 Flora Levy Lecture in the Humanities. But unless someone happened to have read section A, page 29, of *The New York Times* Friday edition, or to have been in Lafayette on the night of his lecture, it

* See especially the articles collected in *Critical Views of Isaac Bashevis Singer* (1969).

is unlike they would have noticed this essay—which not only has value as a window onto Singer's intellectual foundation as a literary figure, but also serves as a testament of faith for anyone struggling to find meaning in the modern world.

Singer never had the opportunity to publish a volume of nonfiction writing during his lifetime. But the essays he translated offer readers insight into the issues that preoccupied him as an author—and how his personal beliefs regarding the world's societies and cultures directly informed the development of his public persona. And while he never fully integrated his intellectual concerns into his popular image as a storyteller, his essays bring to light the web of artistic convictions and Jewish traditions at the base of his fiction. They also offer an unobstructed view onto his attitudes toward, among many other topics, sexuality, vegetarianism, the supernatural, and the unique spirit of Yiddish.

Above all, as a collection, *Old Truths and New Clichés* lays bare Singer's belief in literature's ability to portray those moments when what we think we know collides with what is beyond our understanding.

The Literary Arts

The Satan of Our Time

A Yiddish writer in America is an unseen entity, almost a ghost. Perhaps this is why I am so interested in ghost stories and in the supernatural. I am inclined in all my writings to search for what is hidden from the eye. Somewhere I believe every human being to be possessed, and to me real writers are those who have the ability of exorcism.

My first book, *Satan in Goray,* was published in Warsaw, Poland, in 1935, the year I came to the U.S.A., and since then I have struggled with devils and imps in all my works. I am old-fashioned enough to believe in God too.

Besides writing fiction, I work as a journalist for the *Jewish Daily Forward.* I am married and have a son.

I believe that this generation is possessed by the worst devil the netherworld has ever sent to mislead us. The Satan of our time plays the part of a humanist and has one desire: to save the world. The exorcism of this demon is the most difficult, but I am ready to do my share.

This undated autobiographical note, handwritten in pencil, was found in Singer's archives. It appears to have been prepared as an introduction to a public event. The subject matter as well as the steadiness of Singer's hand suggest that it was jotted down some time in the 1960s.

Journalism and Literature

I know of writers who consider it a tragedy to earn a living from journalism. They claim that it wastes their free time and that journalism is generally harmful to literary creativity. They argue that a journalist becomes accustomed to writing in a hurry and not weighing and measuring every word, and that the means and methods of journalism are altogether contrary to creativity. The experiences of this writer suggest a different approach to the question.

It has been my experience that I wrote my best works in the midst of journalistic hullabaloo, often right in the editorial offices between one article and another. My novels *The Family Moskat* and *The Manor* were published in installments in the *Jewish Daily Forward*, and I virtually prepared a new chapter each week for publication on the following Saturday. It is true that I later reworked them, refined the language and cut, but the bulk of the work was done in a hurry while the editor and the typesetter demanded copy.

Nearly all the great Russian writers published their works in newspapers and magazines. Dostoevsky was an outstand-

This essay first appeared in the *Forverts* as "Zhurnalism un literatur" (Journalism and Literature, March 24, 1965, page 4). It puts into words some of Singer's thoughts on the circumstances and methods of writing that he developed during a lifetime working for a daily newspaper, as well as the cutting and editing taken up after his works first appeared serially in Yiddish.

ing journalist, and while it is true that his literary writings contained journalistic elements, they apparently did no harm. Tolstoy would have surely been a master at journalism had he applied himself to the task. Chekhov wrote almost all his sketches for newspapers. The only well-known Russian writer who avoided the press and sought to isolate himself on islands and in icy palaces was Andreyev, the least important of the Russian masters. In French literature, Maupassant and Zola had close connections with the press, and in American literature, Edgar Allan Poe and Walt Whitman were both journalists.

But it isn't merely a question of experiences and names. I believe that journalism exerts a beneficial influence upon literary creativity because the same laws apply to both.

The first rule of a journalistic piece is that the writer should provide something new. The practice of rehashing old facts is not journalism. The newspaper is an organ of *news*. It may sound paradoxical, but the same holds true in literature, albeit in a broader sense. Every good work of literature must contain an element of *information*. Readers must feel that a writer provides them with some sort of revelation, a fresh approach, a different mood, a new form. We seek news in literature, too, although the concept may be different. A work that offers readers no new outlook, no new facts, new characters—such a work is worthless. Quite frequently, literature introduces us to a new type of society. A good literary work may be compared to a journey to a strange land. The historical novel—if it is a good one—often provides us with new information and a reappraisal of history. Flaubert's *Salammbô* contains a wealth of information. Tolstoy's *War and Peace* possibly revealed nothing new about Napoleon, but it did provide fresh insight into Russian aristocracy and militarism.

Certainly, literature, like journalism, seeks news, and although each does this at a different level, occasionally, they even do so at the *same* level.

Yet there is even a more significant element shared by the two. Good literature, like good journalism, strives to provide facts without superfluous interpretation. If this isn't true today, it has been true until now and, I believe, will be true in the future. It is not incumbent upon authors, nor upon journalists, to interpret every phenomenon they describe, to fit it snugly into the chain of cause and effect. Certainly, they are not obligated to employ psychology, to declare precisely what effect this or that fact had upon their characters. Today, when literature strives so hard to become a branch of psychology, and virtually to impinge upon the functions of the psychoanalyst and the sociologist, my viewpoint may seem old-fashioned. But it is my contention that where literature becomes overly psychological, it loses both its virtues: the literary and the psychological. The so-called psychological writer is a psychologist in literature, and a litterateur in psychology. The great masters of literature adapted themselves to the limitations of the newspaper writer. They gave the facts without concern as to how odd these might appear to the reader. It is a fact, for example, that Dostoevsky never made clear why Raskolnikov, in *Crime and Punishment*, decided to commit murder. Nor did he reveal the reasons for the murders in *The Brothers Karamazov*. He permitted his protagonists to explain their own actions, but the author never did this himself, and Raskolnikov remains an enigma, as actually does every murderer. Someplace I have stated that facts never become outmoded, but commentaries are born already stale.

Yet there is still another important connection between journalism and literature. When scientists have something to say, they reckon little with the patience of their readers. No one expects a physician writing about skin disease to be interesting or entertaining. They keep on writing until their subject is exhausted.

The situation changes completely when it comes to writing news. No matter how important a news item may be, journalists must contend with their readers' patience. Editors of every newspaper reject reams of news copy because in their estimation it would bore readers. News that is boring is not news from the journalistic standpoint, though it may be news by every other standard.

The same is true in literature. No matter how deep a literary work may be, if it bores the reader, it is worthless. In this area, literature goes even beyond journalism. The modern newspaper is made up of different sections for people of divergent interests. The reader of the sports section may not be interested in the financial section, and vice versa. In literature, no sections exist. The *whole* book must interest the reader.

Many writers who fear journalism try—consciously or unconsciously—to sever the natural connections between journalism and literature. To begin with, they are convinced that the function of literature is primarily to analyze or to probe. They don't consider it necessary to provide readers with enough information about the milieu, the physical surroundings, or the mores of their characters. They reject the contention that literature must be interesting. On the contrary, they make a fetish of works that are boring. These are allegedly products of a marriage of literature and science, but actually they are neither. This way, the literature of many modern writers grows more and more concerned with the interpretation of facts—as if facts could be really interpreted.

It's odd that the very writers who have sought so eagerly to divorce themselves from journalism have secretly drawn closer to it. Modern writers who attempt to apply analysis and psychology, to explain the motives of their protagonists, surrender style, end up neglecting form and evolving into incompetent journalists. Analysis demands repetition, but literature must be devoid of repetition. Analysis is wordy, while true literature must be brief and selective. The long books of the masters were long because they were rich in information and color. The modern book that is long is often inflated through repetition. That is the reason the editor plays such a vital role in publishing today. That is why whole chunks are deleted from literary works. Publishers and editors have become the final judges of the lengths of books. In many cases, a modern book becomes worthwhile only after it has been put out in digest form.

Literature has nothing to fear from *good* journalism, since both have much in common. The good writer is almost always also a good journalist.

Why Literary Censorship
Is Harmful

Urbane people who have a preference for what they call "pure" literature and theater have in recent years been shocked by obscene language printed in books and newspapers, and vulgar speech heard in the theater. Those with daughters have especially strong feelings. They somehow cannot imagine them reading and hearing this sort of trash. This obviously concerns what is happening in English, French, German, and other such literatures. Some feel it's foolish to remove virtually all censorship from literature and theater, while keeping a rather strict

This essay first appeared in the *Forverts* as "Farvos a tsenzur oyf literatur iz shedlikh" (Why Censorship of Literature Is Harmful, July 10, 1966), under the byline Yitskhok Bashevis—which was rare, as Singer usually used Varshavski for most of his literary criticism. A partial English translation, credited to B. Chertoff and appearing to be a first draft, was found in the archives bearing no handwritten corrections and missing the first page. Aside from this essay, Singer published several pieces on the topic of censorship—including "'Umanshtendige' reyd un seks in der literatur" ("Indecent" Language and Sex in Literature, April 21, 1963, section 2, page 5), appearing in an English translation by Mirra Ginsburg in *Jewish Heritage* in 1965, as well as "Zol men ingatsn opshafn di tsenzur?" (Should Censorship Be Completely Abolished? Feb. 2, 1965, page 4), for which no translation has been found—both appearing under the name Varshavski. This piece was chosen over the others because, as Singer notes in the piece, he had written about the issue before, and this presents his developed position on the topic. The first two paragraphs, which were missing from the draft in the archive, appear in my translation.

censorship on movies, radio, and television. I have already written on this topic, but the problem is so relevant, that it is necessary to debate the question again.

Everyone knows that the human mouth cannot be censored. People who want to use foul language, tell lies, invent libel, spread gossip, speak ill of others, flatter them, and so on—such people are not afraid of any censorship. Where is there a censor who can hear everything said by humanity? There are nevertheless many people who monitor their own mouths. Foul and corrupt people, underworld types, have their own environment, their own neighborhoods, their own hiding places. Better people want to stay away from them. Even among better people, it often happens that some commit sins of the tongue, but sooner or later public opinion is formed. We know who is kind and who is rude, who tells lies and who the truth. We often treat people according to how they speak or behave.

Lifting the curbs on speech in the theater and literature should not necessarily doom these arts to the nether depths of language and good taste. A free literature and fresh, unfettered literary viewpoint can and must eventually emerge from the removal of censorious restraint. The transition will be very slow—but inevitable. In other words, the fact that writers and playwrights take special license in the use of obscene language without fear of censure under the current condition does not seal the fate of all future plays and books. Countless literary works and theater productions are appreciated and enjoyed, though they are completely free of incidences of the famous four-letter word, or the use of foul language.

This, however, does not mean that the theater and literature should revert to the Victorian Age, with its total abstinence from sexual themes. Those among us who would advocate a "pure" theater and lily-white written page, in which all reference to or suggestions of sex are replaced with "holy" or abridged versions, have long since lost the war. After Freud and the psychological enlightenment that came in the wake of his discoveries, one can no longer look upon sex as "dirty." If sex is "dirty," we are all dirt, spawned by dirt. If sex is "dirty," the Holy Scriptures are written purveyors of dirt, and, therefore, dirty works.

Modern writers and the writers of the future will treat sex as one of the most important factors of the human picture. It is nearly impossible to depict a romance without going into the intimate aspects of the relationship between the people who are its principle characters. Just as difficult is the undertaking of a novel in which love, divorce, jealousy or lust are central to the theme, without any vivid descriptions of the sexual lives of its characters.

We are living in an age of transition. The fact that the power of the censor has been almost completely scrapped is exploited by a great many poor writers and playwrights whose sole aim is to sell their works by offering the reading public shockingly frank sexual passages and scenes, whether they are necessary to the plot or not. Readers will often flock to purchase a book simply because it has gained notoriety through the use of the four-letter word. It is oddly true that dirty words and sexually descriptive passages are often worlds apart. Writers who freely use foul language are often woefully unskilled in depicting a sex scene in an artful manner. Conversely, there are novelists who eschew the use of "free" language in their writing, but are supremely adroit in penning a scene describing, on the most intimate level, a love scene between two people. Dostoevsky, Maupassant, Zola, and Balzac were all masters at the art of unfolding sex scenes by use of subtle nuances and delicately screened wording. One must bear in mind that in none of the ancient literatures handed down through the ages, whether

Hebrew, Sanskrit, or even ancient Greek and Latin, was there any evidence of "dirty" words. The famous writer Henry Miller sent me a Hebrew version of his novel *Tropic of Cancer*. The translated version carried not one "dirty" word, so rampant in the original work. The language used in this Hebrew translation was the very same as that used countless times in the Bible, Gemara, and many texts studied in yeshivas and other citadels of Jewish learning. I recently met Indian writers who assured me that this is also true of Sanskrit.

Oddly, it was once considered improper to use the word "cur" or "bitch." When I undertook to write for the *Forward*, I was advised that Abe Cahan did not allow words such as "lice," "bedbugs," or "syphilis" in his newspaper. He maintained that these expressions were offensive to his readers. Yet the Bible does not hesitate to use the word "lice" or to employ the names of different skin diseases.

There are writers who will not elaborate on a sexual theme or scene. Yet these people do not, through the use of pen and tongue, hesitate to vilify, defame, smear, or otherwise involve others in harmful situations. In the Chofetz Chaim's religious book, *Desirer of Life*, very little is mentioned concerning the use of "dirty" words, but the greatest emphasis is placed on the harm wrought to others by the calumnious evil tongue. Yet this is the area where most people are unguarded and least mindful of the great suffering they can inflict on others. No "dirty" word is so far-reaching in its devastation as the socially accepted word dropped by the evil tongue.

Those who supported Stalin while he wrecked the lives of countless innocents, who enthusiastically upheld him and defended his vicious acts against Jewish writers of the Soviet Union even as he was destroying both the writers and the literature—it is these who sullied their pens and tongues without the use of a single foul word!

I would like to make another observation regarding an important fact with which writers rarely concern themselves.

The so-called "dirty" word has, as every other word in the spoken language, its unique function. When a word is not openly used, but reserved solely for certain private usage, it becomes extremely effective. This is mainly why people refrain from the common use of a word that has its particular place and function. The underworld, through its daily use of ugly language, has blunted and watered down this language's power to shock. Hence arose the need for newer, more provocative "bad" words.

In the Talmud, language and stories are permitted to have a marked effect on mood and spirit. At every turn, they employ words that carry a strong sexual flair. A person who uses belligerent language in daily speech soon loses the power to summon appropriate words with which to berate another person, however at fault the second person may be. Those who employ solemn oaths in their daily speech often find it impossible to muster an oath meaningful enough to be believed by others. A curse that comes from someone who curses all day long loses all power and meaning. The opposite is just as true. An individual given to the use of superlatives in describing every menial thing—words like "fabulous," "wonderful," or "marvelous"—will soon find it difficult to praise the praiseworthy. A skilled cook must know just how much spice and flavoring to add to each dish.

Limiting language is necessary both in the world of literature and in our daily speech. Indiscriminate use of a word weakens its meaning. Yet when used in the proper context and with correct emphasis, words can produce a hypnotic effect.

People in high places must, by virtue of their responsibility to others, be extremely guarded in their speech. The head of a country dare not indulge in the same angry outbursts against another dignitary as the vulgar columnist. Doing so might very well result in a war. When controls on speech are dropped, words no longer serve us. They cannot, therefore, be expected to do the masterful job of effective and forceful articulation. Reporting or recounting becomes an extremely difficult task.

In these word-laden times, people have almost surrendered the privilege of expressing exact thought through effective speech. Ugly words have lost their ugliness through repetition. Beautiful words have been stripped of their freshness through familiarity. Fortunately, there are still countless people who reject the lie, the evil expression, the twisted and malicious phrase. It is they who uphold the weight and might of the true word. As champions of the true word, they engender respect and admiration in others. Without these standard-bearers of truth through speech, human expression would become useless, even mute, notwithstanding the fact that our dictionaries are growing ever fuller.

It is a commonly known fact that in the period following the Russian Revolution, capitalism was the constant target of all the venom the Russian newspapers could muster. That day is long past. Today, *Pravda* and *Izvestia* are guarded in their language. The growing strength of Russia and its desire to cooperate with other world powers has given rise to this renewed moderation.

Irresponsible and reckless language is the folly of those who feel no moral or social obligation to others and who choose to disregard its cost to themselves. Their praise is as worthless as their abuse. They feel no compunction in making complete reversals whenever one is deemed expedient, or when it might yield an advantage. These people have lost the greatest gift bestowed upon humanity—*speech*—the gift of communication.

We must conclude that the job of guarding speech cannot be delegated to a censor. People must ultimately be their own censors. Moreover, "dirty" words are but a small and relatively innocuous part of the dirt that unethical people let loose from their lips.

I hardly believe that people in the future will relax their vigil in the interest of decent and socially acceptable speech. It is more probable that, with the growth of a higher culture and increased belief in loftier ideals, greater beauty in expression will come together with a stronger desire to elevate the human word to its highest level.

Who Needs Literature?

There are times when I wonder what purpose fiction serves today. Why fabricate plots when life unfolds an inexhaustible wealth of events, stranger than anything literature might offer? Fantasy will never be able to match all the surprising twists that make up facts. No writer's pen has been able to produce a work so true and free of imperfections as a case history, or the proceedings of a courtroom. Just as there is no perfect crime, so there is no perfect novel. Even *Anna Karenina* and *Madame Bovary* reveal flaws and inconsistencies that are part of all fiction.

I am sometimes afraid that, sooner or later, humanity will arrive at the conclusion that reading fiction is a waste of time. But why should this thought frighten me? Is it just because, as a writer, I would be one of the victims?

It's not just this. Fiction represents a highly intellectual challenge. Even if a machine could be invented that would be capable of relating to us the experiences of a new Raskolnikov, a modern Madame Bovary, or an American Anna Karenina, it

The Yiddish original of this essay appeared in the *Forverts* in three installments— "Tsu vos literatur?" (Who Needs Literature? Oct. 20, 1963, section 2, page 5), "Keyn shum shrayber shraybt nit 'far'n shufald'" (Writer's Don't Write "For the Drawer," Nov. 3, 1963, section 2, page 5), and "Vos iz di tsukunft fun dem kinstlerishn vort?" (What Is the Future of the Artistic Word? Nov. 17, 1963, section 2, page 5). Although the title "Old Truths and New Clichés" was first created and used for a different essay, a later draft of this piece bears this title as well.

would still be interesting to find out what happened to our imagination and its age-old instrument: the pen.[1]

As a matter of fact, it would be a lot more difficult for us to make peace with a literary machine than with a computer dealing with numbers. If a machine could tell stories and write plays, creative people would have nothing to live for, nothing to expect.

Just the same, there already exist a number of forces that might gradually lead up to this situation. As modern readers learn more about psychology and human behavior, the commentaries of literary critics will seem to them more and more superfluous, erroneous, or obsolete. Even now, there is little in a novel that can surprise them. They can get it all from case histories, newspapers and magazines, from the radio, from television, and from the big screen. A person who walks from New York to California in our time may evoke admiration, yet walking is not taken seriously as a means of long-distance transportation. Fiction may become a playful sport for amateurs. We already see it happening in poetry.[2] It is often so oblique and obscure, so conceptual and nonessential, that it has become a jargon for the few who imagine that they possess the key to solve its riddles.

Thus far theater has not reached this phase, but it is getting there fast. The novel, we are told, is doing well. But many of the works that are sold as novels turn out to be more journalism than literature.

Never before has the dividing line between journalism and literature been as tenuous as it is now.[3] In Chelm they called water sour cream, but this did not make their blintzes taste better. To designate journalistic writings as novels represents neither a revolution nor an artistic gain. It is no more than a mask used to conceal the fact that prose literature now is going through the same crisis as poetry, though often in a different direction. Modern fiction seems to have forgotten its essence and purpose.

Every type of amnesia has its causes, and the literary amnesia of our time is no exception. The small number of true talents that arise in any one generation is no longer enough to feed the many publishing houses, the huge printing presses, and the masses of readers that have developed with the decline of illiteracy. Moreover, true talents no longer have either the force or the means to make the same impression on their readers as they once did. But instead of admitting that literature is losing ground, some critics, publishers, and often authors themselves simply set about to alter the concept of literature—to broaden it, as it were. What actually happens is that they muddle the true meaning of the term "literature." This is comparable to a situation in which a group of athletes decide that the runners in a foot race would be allowed to use bicycles. It is a type of revolution that does not serve to enrich the field in which it takes place but actually impoverishes and destroys it.

It is strange that in our age of specialization, when every science is carefully defined—because every subdivision requires the full attention of a specialist—there should have evolved in fiction a conglomeration, an eclectic hodgepodge of means and methods. Many works of modern fiction include amateurish essays on psychology and sociology, a lot of journalistic material that could be found in newspapers, magazines, and encyclopedias, and a plethora of pseudo-scientific theories and even ideas gleaned from political pamphlets. In some instances neither the writers nor their critics have any idea of what is original and what is borrowed, where writers are moved by their own powers and where they have copied others.[4]

How did poetry reach this state? What has happened to the theater? Why did prose literature transgress its natural "boundaries"?

The real cause for this situation is the fact that the essence of fiction, the study of character and individuality, was never really in great demand. Even when fiction was at its best, there were many readers who would read it for elements that are only of secondary importance. In the days when there were few mass circulation newspapers and no national magazines—and when history books were badly written—readers would seek and find in literature a lot more than what is essential. Literature would be read as a source of information on many subjects. *War and Peace,* for example, would be read as an account of the Napoleonic Wars. The novel could serve as a travelogue or a text on etiquette. At one time, literature provided average readers with their sole contact with psychology and psychiatry.[5]

Modern times have brought about a radical change in this respect. Now readers have unlimited access to information.[6] They can easily attend lectures on these subjects. They can watch travelogues or they can do the traveling themselves. If novels and plays are to survive,[7] they must either take on more and more elements which are foreign to them, or else they must find an audience with a clear interest in character and individuality. But audiences of this caliber are almost as rare as true artists.

Just because people in modern times are surrounded by a veritable deluge of information on every subject, much more should be required of genuine artists today in the way of concentration on the portrayal of character and individuality. But the description of character demands extraordinary talent.

Modern authors who takes literature seriously must steer clear of thousands of events and sentiments which perhaps were justified once, but are a burden today. They find their road more and more blocked with clichés or used material. They must even avoid portraying sincere emotions if these add nothing to the description of character. They cannot afford to get involved in psychological commentaries or sociological guesswork.[8] Instead of being able to draw on a wide choice of nuances of speech, true artists must confine themselves to those word-pictures and images which in their opinion are unique and which help reveal personality.

Strange though this may sound, genuine writers of fiction must pay more attention to what they must not say than to what they may express in their work. They must constantly set themselves limits. Outsiders may think that such authors are retreating or regressing. But like the chess game of today, the game of literature consists more in *avoiding* pitfalls than in creating literary spectacles. The task of avoiding clichés—factual as well as verbal—is well nigh impossible. However much one human being may be different from another, people have a great deal in common, and, given certain situations, they react in the same way. What writers must be careful about is not to create the kinds of situations that would call for clichés and generalizations. They must remember that their object is not humanity as a whole but a single person or a few people, a single situation— events and conditions that will never occur again. A story is not an example but a unique item in the history of humanity.

It is not an easy thing to preach limits in an epoch of so-called literary expansion or explosion. In addition, these limits must be worked out by the authors themselves. In all the profusion of literary criticism today, storytelling is becoming a forgotten art. I don't know of a critic who has tried to call back literature to its natural frontiers. Modern literary criticism has become so involved in psychology and sociology that it has forgotten that literature has laws of its own.

The sphere of the literary artist is individuality, the uniqueness and distinction inherent in human nature, in humanity's destiny and in the circumstances in which people live. No one will deny that there is more to link people together than there is to set them apart. But only that which sets them apart is the final concern of the literary artist. Science—including history, psychology, and psychiatry—is engaged in a never-ending quest for generalizations, for a formula, a law. Artists, on the other hand, deliberately set out to search for that which occurs only once. Art's aim is to provide the insight that, just as no two fingerprints are identical, so no two characters or destinies can be alike. Pornography is not art because it deals with sex in general, not with unique events. Neither are many of the tales about the cruelties of war, starvation, revolution, mass rebellion, or terror. These tales touch our hearts, but they don't give us the sublime gifts art can offer. If art has anything at all to teach us, it is the fact that "in the beginning, there was the exception."

This is the road of literary artists and of every other form of art. But artists cannot achieve this end by direct means. The media at their disposal are not personal in character. The word, which is the writer's medium, is anything but specific. The term "table" can refer to all kinds of tables all over the world, and "love" can be used to describe a great many types of affection. With words, which have no individuality and which are subjected to constant wear and tear, writers must create something unique. They do this through constant observation of human behavior and finding new combinations in which to employ the word. The words may be outworn, but the possibilities for combinations are inexhaustible.

Seen from a purely mathematical angle, the number of such possible combinations is infinite. Some symbolists actually try to make use of this mathematical infinity. But symbols without observation are not enough to bring out character. Literary artists must adhere to nature. They cannot paint their pictures by heart. The symbol is no more than the culmination of a work of art. Actually, the very character of the symbol is scientific rather than individualistic. The artistic symbol must serve as a bridge between the individual and the general, but not as a method of creativity. This is a truth which many adherents of symbolism have overlooked.

The task of prose writers, briefly stated, is to avoid outworn phrases and at the same time not to overlook the living human being. To skim over as swiftly as possible that which is common to all, and to stress the unique element instead. To make use of knowledge without becoming a pseudo-scientist, a sociologizer, a psychologizer, or even a moralist. To strive for symbolic effect without getting involved in symbolism. And to be original while using a language that is clear and intelligible.

The worst mistake a writer can make is to assume that the days of aesthetic enjoyment have passed and that artists can permit themselves to bore their audience in the name of some higher purpose. There is no paradise to compensate bored readers. In art, as in sex, the act and the enjoyment go together. If there is redemption in literature, it must be immanent. In contrast to politics, art does not thrive on promises. It may pay little, but it is all in cash. If it does not impress you now, it never will.

The great number of guides to literary works being published shows the pernicious effect that pretentious criticism has had on so-called literary readers. It is very bad if a reader needs a guide in order to understand Maupassant or Chekhov. Actually, those authors whose works cannot be enjoyed without commentaries and explanations are not worth the commentator's efforts. Our era has seen the rise of a type of writer whose boring personality is hidden behind riddles. Deciphering riddles may be pleasurable to some pedantic minds—but it does not afford artistic enjoyment.

Human individuality is not discovered by tricks of speech. Real writers restrict the volume of words they use while broadening the meaning of those words. They start out with general statements, and proceed from there to a description of the characters and their specific situations. As they proceed, writers must remember that their work has to evoke a sense of enjoyment in readers, to lift their spirit and to give them the means of escape that every form of true art affords, be it comedy or tragedy. Literary artists cannot probe into human individuality without limits. They cannot solve social problems or try to reform society. They are not teachers but basically tellers of tales. They have power, but it is a force without a vector. Terrible as these words may sound, writers are entertainers in the highest sense of the word. They can only touch those truths which evoke interest, amusement, and tension. True artists must have a sense of proportion. They cannot, like scientists, proceed directly and with a single purpose. In art, a truth which is boring is not true.

The idea that writers can write just for themselves is nothing more than an excuse for those who have nothing to write about. The sole standard by which any literary work can be gauged is the readers' reactions—the pleasures they derive or the pains they enjoy. True, there are vulgar or perverted readers. True, there have always been writers who were not appreciated by their contemporaries. But then who eventually discovers them? Only readers.[9] Esoteric writers may decide to aim their writing at a minority. But they cannot talk to themselves forever or search for some truth in which no one else is interested.

It is no mere accident that many of the great masters of literature addressed themselves directly to readers. They saw their audiences before their eyes. Sometimes they would even apologize to their readers because it seemed to them that they were exceeding their limits and that readers might lose patience.

Solipsism is not art. Artists must assume that other people *do* exist. Fiction writers are not creators of ideals or explainers of facts. What they discover must not only be true—it has to possess beauty. There is no such thing as ugly art. If it is ugly, it is not art. If it only disturbs, it is nothing more than a disturbance. If it tries to guide, to analyze social events without regard to proportion and beauty—to structure and to rhythm—it is lost from the very beginning.[10]

One of the false doctrines proclaimed by some literary criticism is that form is all-important and plot of secondary concern. Actually, form and plot cannot be considered apart from one another. The essayism that has invaded modern literature, the forced sophistry and self-analysis, are often attempts to conceal the lack of a plot. The same applies to those stilted stage productions that have no true drama. The fact that pulp writers fabricate cheap "suspense" is not an argument against genuine suspense. Without suspense there can be no literature. If readers are not eager to find out what will happen next, or if they know the outcome in advance, they don't have a story at all. In literature, any surprise is better than no surprise. Interesting evil is of more value than trite holiness. Literature often likes sickness better than it likes health. Literature is not always on the side of the just. It does not always believe in equality. It loves freedom but it is a special kind of freedom: the freedom of the human caprice and the whim.

It certainly is not my intention here to preach realism, mysticism, or any other literary "ism." I do believe in literary experimentation—and that there is room for a great many schools of literature. I am sure that there are new media and methods still to be developed in writing. All creative writers bring their own variations on style and method to their work. But I do not believe that the maximum can be attained by discarding the minimum: namely, by broadening the definition of literature to such an extent that its outlines become blurred, or by constricting it to a degree that it becomes a puzzle.

There is yet another point which I would like to raise. Within the past few years the view has been spread that talent is a term without meaning, that it represents an outworn concept—a metaphysical concept. Modern people don't like to deal with things that can't be measured, weighed, photographed, or analyzed in a laboratory. Many feel that the concept of "talent" belongs in the realm of parapsychology. According to the classic definition, talent is a quality with which a person is born. Those who believe that character and personality are molded *entirely* by environment have no patience with the "old-fashioned" concept of talent. But neither Lysenko nor others of his kind will ever be able to cancel the role of heredity in art.

The most important manifestations of talent are an innate and never-relenting urge to brood about the eternal questions: a refusal to accept human and animal suffering. Individualism is the very air that talented people breathe. Whatever they want to create must be their own creation. They may be loved by many, but they are not leaders of the masses. No matter how deeply they are rooted in their environment, they will never be truly a part of it. They will always be the exception. They belong and do not belong to the society in which they live. True talent wrestles not so much with social orders as with God. Talented people are often pessimists or even fatalists. But they cannot be atheists for the simple reason that by their very nature they must wrangle with the higher powers. They may revile God, but they cannot *deny* God.

This is why no dictators or social revolutionaries have ever succeeded in harnessing talent for their purposes.[11]

I do not envy the true artists of the future. They may face even more difficulties than Dostoevsky, Edgar Allan Poe, and Van Gogh. They may be forced to fight against triteness that appears in the trappings of originality. They may have to do battle with cruelty that that preaches humanity. In a planned economy, they may even be altogether restrained from self-expression. Nevertheless, I believe that true art cannot vanish. Genuine talent is endowed with a force that no one can destroy.[12]

Within the past century, philosophy has become so analytical, so self-critical and so overly self-conscious, that it has almost committed suicide. I do not think that art will meet with the same fate. I believe that art, expressed in the written word, will yet rear edifices of astounding beauty and harmony.

Upon the ruins of banal trash, shallow psychology, false sociology, and empty symbolism and formalism, there will rise an art pure in character. It will reveal those surprises that are found nowhere except in the human personality, its struggles and its growth. Real art touches the thing in itself, the very essence of being and creation.

As it entertains, art keeps on searching for the eternal truths in its own fashion. It still tries to penetrate the essence of being, to solve the riddle of time and change, to find an answer to suffering, to reveal love in the very abyss of cruelty and injustice. True artists can never make peace with death and oblivion. They know that we are fragments in God's unending book, moments in eternity. Our hopes are closely connected with all the stars, all the galaxies of the cosmos. If the universe is an accident, so are we. If the universe makes sense, so do we. This is the message both of religion and art.

Old Truths and New Clichés

Is it possible for art not to look to nature and to learn from it? Before we can answer this question, we must clarify the question itself.

In a broad sense, nobody—and especially no artist—can run away from nature. Writers who think up impossible and false situations, painters who paint abstract pictures, sculptors who create figures that have no resemblance to existing objects, composers who compose symphonies that have no rhythm or

This essay appeared in three installments—"Ongenumene kinsterlishe emesn vos zaynen falsh" (Accepted Artistic Truths that Are False, Nov. 19, 1967, section 2, page 5), "Ven di kunst vil ton dos ummeglikh" (When Art Tries to Do the Impossible, Nov. 26, 1967, section 2, page 5), and "Di kunst in unzer tsayt" (Art in Our Time, Dec. 3, 1967, section 2, page 5). This piece is especially challenging from an editorial perspective because text from this work appears in various versions and stages. The only complete version in English appears in an early draft. Later edits appear on drafts that exist only as typescript fragments. One of those fragments incorporates an earlier essay, "Der barg-aroyf un barg-arop in der kunst" (Ups and Downs in Art, Dec. 10, 1961, section 2, page 5)—of which there are, also, only fragments available. Yet these fragments are crucial because they contain corrections that thematize the central idea in this essay—the notion that "old truths" are discarded in contemporaneity for "new clichés." Indeed, it is in the last edit, available only in fragments, that Singer's English-language handwriting is shown striking out the first installment's original title—"Accepted Artistic Truths Which Are False"—then writing "Old Clichés," and then, again, crossing out "Clichés" and adding "Truths and New Clichés," giving the essay its full title. Early drafts of this essay credit Faygah Mark and Linda R. Portnoy as translators.

harmony—they all are united with nature. People, with their fantasies, caprices, and idiosyncrasies, are all a part of nature. Spinoza maintained that there can be no false ideas, but only crippled ideas. People who say that two and two equal five actually mean that they are four, only they do not use the correct words. In our dreams, we often see things that are contrary to our experience, against logic, and yet dreams are a part of human nature. What, then, do we mean by art that does not learn from nature?

By this we mean art that is thoroughly subjective, which concerns itself only with the human spirit—its caprices, fantasies, and mistakes—ignoring or distorting what goes on in the so-called objective world. For hundreds of years, European science abandoned experience and delved into the wisdom of Aristotle. The artists of that time wrote on themes dealing with the *Iliad* and the *Odyssey* or the Bible, and totally overlooked their own time and environment. Certainly, they did not abandon nature, but they went around and around in circles with the texts and with authorities that already existed.[1] They chewed the cud that had long since been digested.[2] If science and literature had continued on this path, we would have had no Newton, Darwin, Flaubert, Edison, Tolstoy, Gogol, or Dostoevsky. Perhaps mathematics and logic would have progressed. For these, observation is not necessary.

We live, now, in a time when many artists are beginning to turn, more and more, to themselves alone, to their own spirit, their own dreams and moods. The great admiration and imitation of Kafka, the enthusiasm that modern critics shows for Joyce, the way that modern poetry increasingly becomes a language only poets can understand (or not understand), or that abstract painters disregard the object and concern themselves only with combinations of forms and colors—all this shows that art is tired of the outside world.

There are many reasons for these phenomena—social, psychological, perhaps even political. Many artists feel that the outside world does not have anything left to teach them. What will come from describing yet another environment, or from painting more portraits or landscapes? They believe that if art is to have depth, it must become basically solipsistic. Even scientists often display a weariness of observing nature.[3] Science has gathered millions of facts that people can and must ignore. Many humanists argue that the key to the human dilemma lies in humanity itself.[4] No new experience can bring with it peace between nations or races, economic equality, or justice.[5]

It is characteristic for art that is involved in its own self to become intellectual, oversensitive to form, self-conscious about style.[6] Originality stops being that which it must be—a natural attribute of the creator—and becomes, instead, a method, a challenge, a product of conscious effort. Many modern creations have nothing but the kind of originality that is a result of a trick, a distortion, or sometimes a joke.[7] At no time did the true masters try to be original. Originality was a product of their personality.[8]

True artists are never against[9] experimenting with form and construction.[10] But history shows that where originality becomes the creator's aim, art loses its power.[11] It is an irony of art history that those who place the most emphasis on originality soon become the epigones. Those who try *only* to look inward cease to see themselves, and those who wish to teach the public do not teach and do not entertain. The efforts of such pseudo-art are directed in a number of directions, but I will speak mainly about literature.

Writers who believe that literature is a branch of psychology often remain psychologists in literature and litterateurs in psychology. Good novels contain a lot of facts about human behavior, but when literature builds its structure on Freud or any psychological master, it must fail. A great number of modern novels are sadly similar to the tales of those who are psychoanalyzed. This type of novel is a mixture of a confession and a boast.[12] On the whole, "case histories" cannot be a substitute for artful stories. No story writer can compete with the case histories we find in the writings of Krafft-Ebing, Forel, Block, and many Freudians, Adlerians, and Jungians. If readers want facts, they do not read novels. The same is true of sociology. Readers do not read a novel because they want to acquaint themselves with the social and political conditions of a certain country or part of the world. Literary masterpieces contain elements of psychology and sociology, but no one reads Tolstoy to be acquainted with agrarian problem in Russia, or *Crime and Punishment* to learn about criminal psychology. The chapters in *Anna Karenina* and *War and Peace* where Levin or Pierre discuss the problems of the Russian peasants are the most boring parts of these novels. *Crime and Punishment* gives us the psychology of one specific criminal, a unique case in the history of criminology. Raskolnikov is not an archetype, but a character, and one can learn little from his behavior about criminology in general.[13]

Another misunderstanding in literature is the effort to free it of all inhibitions,[14] and in this way to enlarge the territory of literature.[15] I am absolutely in favor of eliminating censorship. No one can exactly point to the place where literature ends and pornography begins. But writers who misuse this freedom have contributed little to the literature of our time. Foul language and sex are not synonyms.[16] Most of the modern sex novels are sexless—they do not affect the reader.[17] The writers of these sex novels and sex plays[18] are so preoccupied with their attempt to shock readers that they forget the novel has to have[19] characters. A desire to be psychological, sociological, rebellious, and shocking has driven many modern writers into a type of artistic amnesia. Modern writers envy science and scientists. They want to be like a new Freud or Marx, and often a combination of both. They dream of establishing a scientific school, and even of changing the world with their work. Many writers of war novels had the illusion that, through their descriptions of war atrocities, they could lead the world to peace, as if the reader did not know what war was.[20] The army-camp novel, or novels that describe unemployment, exploitation, and social rebellion, have contributed nothing toward the improvement of the working class.[21] Literature must be informative, but no one reads novels to gain information. Literature deals with particulars, from which one cannot learn about the general. In addition, literature is a force that has no direction.[22] True literature always gives the thesis and the antithesis, the hope and the disappointment. It is often pessimistic and fatalistic. It awakens and puts to sleep. All of German literature could not withstand the propaganda of a single Goebbels. A large number of political writers are conservative—notwithstanding the fact that they describe all the sufferings and injustice of their environment. It is a fact that neither communism, fascism, nor even liberalism has found a reflection in the literature of our time.

In my own environment, neither Zionism nor socialism has found a real reflection in Yiddish or Hebrew literature. Many Zionists and socialists had bitter complaints against authors who stood aside while an entire people was making such historical efforts. But literature could not push the wagon of Jewish history, just as it could not push the wagon of world history. Not one novel has emerged in Russia that is both artistic and captures the spirit of Bolshevism.

Art has been and remains a medium of entertainment. Modern artists fear this word.[23] They feel that it is disgraceful to be entertainers. They want to be teachers, leaders, and discoverers, but this they are not and can never be.

If Homer had written the *Iliad* and the *Odyssey* to teach the world about Greek history and mythology, both works would have long been forgotten. Readers would have been immediately forgotten Homer if he had tried to interpret events according to the psychology or the philosophy of his time, or even to preach morals or pacifism. Homer was a bard, an entertainer, and this is why his works live today—this is why they are so rich in information and in history.

Shakespeare's greatness is based on his ability to write for the theater of his time—to amuse the public of the Globe Theater. This is true of all literary geniuses.

Tolstoy's literary decline began when he decided to teach neo-Christian ideas in his works, though it was a slow decline from great heights.

Notwithstanding those clichés from which some modern writers seek to run away, they are more possessed by clichés than writers before them. Modern prose writers can no longer tell a story. Their prose is all patches.[24] The modern novel is really a collection of stories and interpretations.[25] Very many contemporary writers do not portray their characters, but write essays about them. Some modern prose writings are a combination of fiction and criticism. They offer both the fable and the moral. They state a fact and explain it.[26] More and more, literature is becoming the psychoanalysis and the sociology of the dilettante.

The greatest tragedy of modern literature is that so many writers have lost their faith in higher powers. They speak of God, but they do not *believe* in God. Neither do they believe in the devil.

Virtually all of them are skeptics, or not even that. Writers in the nineteenth century regarded the world from the point of view of good and evil, virtue and sin, God and Satan. Contemporary writers have no ideological foundation, or else their ideologies are built on social theories. It is impossible to write truthfully about human beings without having faith in something higher than human beings. Present-day writers see humanity as the highest authority. Humanity is virtually their idol, though they also despise it. This is the paradox of faithlessness.

Modern art is terribly afraid of the cliché, but while running away from the old and sometimes wise clichés—actually old and eternal truths—it is cursed with a multitude of new clichés.* One of the popular clichés is the one about the "Angry Young Man."[27] This carries into art something with which it has a very limited relationship.[28] The anger of an artist, if it exists at all, has a totally different nature than that of a revolutionary. Real artists have grievances toward God and toward the higher powers. They are wise enough to know that[29] human character is eternal and no social upheaval can change it basically. The anger of a Strindberg and the anger of a Lenin are of completely different natures.

Another cliché taken over from sociology—actually from the popular pamphlet—is the idea that there can and must be a cosmopolitan art. We speak today of the international novel and international drama. There is no international novel. Art is, in its essence, national.[30] It is deeply connected with a land, a locality, a group. It must have its roots in folklore. It must have an address.

---

* The section that starts with the words "Modern prose writers can no longer tell a story" and ends with the words "cursed with a multitude of new clichés" is taken from existing fragments of "Ups and Downs in Literature." In Singer's drafts, these paragraphs are incorporated into the essay directly through handwritten corrections.

Art becomes internationally recognized only because it is tied in with a specific group and a specific culture. When it makes an attempt to be cosmopolitan, it ceases to exist. This appears to be outstandingly true in literature, but it is also true in every other art form. The limitations of many abstract painters lie in the fact that they are associated with no group. They express humanity in general and, because of this, their art is merely decorative.

The old painters and sculptors were truly united with groups, provinces, and eras.[31]

Many of the plastic artists of our time have almost discarded the portrait, although it has always been a source of artistic individuality. They tremble in deadly fear of telling a story. The fear of painting being narrative is almost as great as the opposition to narrative poetry. Modern artists increasingly lose the power to tell a story, although stories are the backbone of every art.[32]

In all art forms, the opinion now reigns that beauty and art have little in common. Beauty is an outmoded and mystical concept. What is beautiful? Scientific language cannot define beauty and, therefore, it is disqualified. The complaint is that life is not beautiful, and a beautiful art is, therefore, a denial of life. Nowhere can a greater falsehood be found. Art must have beauty. Ugly art is just as false a concept as tedious art.

It is true that human life is often ugly, but we do not read books and we do not visit museums to add to the feeling of ugliness and tedium. We do not read poetry to find in it chaos, formlessness, and disharmony.[33] Actually, though one cannot nearly define beauty or inborn talent, both are the elements that comprise a work of art.[34] The expression *belles lettres* is not an anachronism. All great works had in them harmony, rhythm, and proportion. They had no need of any "guide" to enable them to be enjoyed. They were often accessible to everyone.[35]

When art becomes exceptionally difficult and inaccessible, this is a sign that artists have lost themselves.[36] No commentary can make *Finnegan's Wake* a real work of art.

Originality cannot be made to order. Originality stems from a unique character, not from concentrating greatly on form and technique. Originality[37] is an accompanying phenomenon of art, not its goal.[38] The true artist is at all times steeped in tradition and in folklore. One can even say that the originality of the masters appears *against* their will. No technical inventions can cover up a banal personality.[39]

There is not and can never be in art, as in nature, revolutions or even a straightforward evolution. If evolution exists at all in art, it goes hand-in-hand with the very slow evolution of character and personality.[40] The triumph of one talent cannot be overtaken by those who come later. In art, there is no such thing as a midget who stands on the shoulders of a giant. In art, the midget is always standing on firm ground.[41] There are no milestones in art. There are no standard methods. Nobody can foresee what a character's genetics will produce. One can imagine a generation of the highest scientific achievements existing simultaneously with the lowest art, or the opposite.

Just as a plant must have earth and water to grow, artists must cleave to their personal environment, their youth, the folklore of their land, and the juices that feed the fantasies of their people. There are no international artists, and there are no[42] artists who create entirely from themselves. Artists, like plants, must have roots, and the deeper the soil, the deeper the roots. Art is the opposite of analysis.[43] Sometimes, five-year-old "wunderkinds" show great powers in mathematics. But there is no prodigy in literature or painting—not even in composition.[44] At the moment when art tears itself away from its soil, it becomes technical, difficult, pretentious, and tedious.

The achievement of every artist is a one-time occurrence and it exhausts itself in its effort. Artists cannot learn from their own past. Like lovers, they are at all times in danger of failing. But, when they succeed, they produce something that brings others enjoyment, forgetfulness, a feeling of unearthly pleasure, and an insight into the powers that created[45] the world.[46]

Storytelling and Literature

I am going to speak about the importance of storytelling and literature. Actually, to say that storytelling is important to literature is like saying that food is necessary for human beings. Of course, everybody knows it. Take away the story and there is no literature. I am sorry that a number of writers have forgotten this simple fact. Sometimes people forget axioms, things that are so clear to all of us, and fall into a kind of amnesia. It is possible that maybe one day people may even forget that food is necessary for life!

This has happened to literature in our time—but it should not. Why did it happen? Because a number of writers came to the conclusion that instead of telling stories that happened some time ago—yesterday, a week, or a hundred years before—we should instead plan the future. We should write novels about how to build a Communist society, a Socialist society, a Zionist society—all kinds of societies. They began to feel that what happened in the past was not as important. The main thing is what will happen in the future—and the writer is just the person to do this. It was a very big mistake.

For sixty years, critics in the Soviet Union tried to bring about a literature that would truly plan the future. They wanted

No Yiddish original has been found for this essay and no date appears on the English-language version. The title is taken from the first sentence.

their writers to write novels about Stalinism and other kinds of "isms": about how to build a just society or at least a society that listens to every word dictated by Comrade Stalin. Writers were willing because they were afraid. They were told: if you are not going to write novels like these, and this kind of poetry, we will imprison you and say that you are an enemy of the people. We'll put you in Lubyanka or some other prison. But even though these writers were willing to do it, and tried their best, they never succeeded because literature is not a means of propaganda. This does not mean that literature does not have ideas and ideals. They are there. But you cannot sit down at your desk and write a novel to enhance socialism, Zionism, communism, liberalism, or any other ism. Because it is not in the nature of the storyteller. Literature *is* storytelling—and you cannot tell a story about the future.

I think about George Orwell's *1984*. He succeeded in a way— but it was not really literature. It was predicting the future. Still, he did not really predict as well as he thought. The wonderful thing about time and the future is that you can never outsmart it, you can never be cleverer than time. We cannot foresee what will happen, neither a hundred years from now, nor even today. Every day before I get my mail I try to guess what kind of letter I am going to get, and it has never happened that I guessed right! Somehow time has a way of doing it differently—and that is what is wonderful about time. I say this in connection with the fact that literature is suddenly compelled to plan or predict the future. But then it becomes too limp and stops being literature.

People often ask me: How do you sit down to write a story, and what are the conditions you need to write a story? And I say that I need three conditions.

One condition is a condition that Aristotle—the great philosopher—already spoke about more than two thousand years ago. He said you must have a story. And not only must you have a story, you must have a story with a beginning, a middle, and an end. This man who made many mistakes in philosophy, physics, and chemistry was very clever when it came to literature. And he really said what a writer must have. Many writers of our generation have forgotten this Aristotelian rule.

In my case, not only must I have a story—which means a topic or theme for a story—but I must also have a passion for writing this story. Sometimes I have a very good topic but somehow I don't have the desire to write it. I never really find out why I don't have the desire. And there is no reason to find out. If you sit down to eat and don't have an appetite for the food, this is already a very good reason not to eat it! Sometimes people force themselves to eat, or force themselves not to eat, which is also a mistake. Because if you have an appetite for something, there is no reason why you should not eat it!

Then there is a third condition that is very important in my writing—a very difficult condition that Aristotle did not tell me about but which I told myself. I must be convinced or at least have the illusion that I am the only one who can write this particular story. This is a very difficult condition because I don't know all the writers in the world. Who knows if there are other writers who can write the same kind of story! But by process of elimination I have learned to tell what I can do and what others can do. If I write a story about a Hasidic family in Warsaw who lived on Krochmalna Street, I somehow know that, let's say, Graham Greene is not going to write it. He didn't live there—not on Krochmalna Street and not nearby—and neither did he live among Hasidim. I can, in the same way, predict that a number of Swedish writers are not going to write about this. After pondering these things for a while, I say to myself: this particular story, I think, is my story, because I am the only one who could write it. It is not only because of the topic but also because of the point of view, the emotions connected with this story, and my own genes, which are certainly not the same as those of any other writer. This rule is my own—I don't tell others who try to write that they should also make this rule for themselves.

In my case, I am a Yiddish writer and I know almost all the Yiddish writers—exactly what they can and cannot do. But for those, let's say, who write in English or Swedish or French, it would be a very difficult condition. They don't know all the Swedish writers and they don't know what they can do—and certainly if you write in English you don't know all the English writers in Australia or wherever they are. But I would say that it is good for writers to give themselves this kind of rule. No matter how difficult it is. When I study literature, let's say the great literature—of the Russians, of the French, or of other nations—I know that somehow every one of them has written a story which the other couldn't write. I read *Anna Karenina* and I admire the story and ask myself: Could Dostoevsky have written *Anna Karenina?* And I am sure that he couldn't. First of all, *Anna Karenina* takes place mostly in Moscow, not in Petersburg, while almost everything Dostoevsky wrote, like *Crime and Punishment*, happens in Petersburg. But it is not only a question of whether the story takes place in Petersburg or Moscow. There are, I could tell you, plenty of reasons why Dostoevsky could not have written *Anna Karenina* and also why Tolstoy, great as he was, never could have written *Crime and Punishment* or *The Brothers Karamazov*.

So this condition is not really so difficult. The principle behind it is that real writers write about things, people, and topics they know best. They never venture out and try something else. I heard one writer tell me many times: *I would be a writer if I went to China for a year. I could come back with a wonderful*

Chinese novel. And I said to the man that, had he done it, he could have only fooled me and not a Chinese person. Someone from China would see, on every page, that he was a stranger to this topic—that he does not write like someone from China.

The same thing is true about literature in general. Sometimes I ask myself: Why *can't* someone go to China for a year and come back with a Chinese novel? My answer is that the very basis of literature is individuality—and individuality is not something that can be shared. No matter who you are, no matter how common your desires may be—food, sex, love—somehow you are never the same person as someone else. Your neighbor or your enemy or your friend, whoever they are, are different. God Almighty has managed to create millions of billions of people in the history of humanity—and all of them had fingerprints. And somehow we know that none of their fingerprints were completely identical with those of another. So if God could do this, if God could create so many people at the same time and make everyone's fingers different, it means that individuality is essential to creation.

You sit down and write. You cannot just write a novel about a certain human being, but, just as when you write a letter, you have to give this human being an address. You write an address to Mr. So-and-So living in Stockholm on Such-and-Such Street. You want the letter to reach this person. The same is true when we write about human beings. You have to get their fingerprints on paper. I don't mean the literal fingerprints, I mean the prints of their spirit, their very nature. Despite the many things we have in common, we are all very different. And this is the wonder of creation.

It is also the wonder of creativity. Since individuality is the essence of creativity, it is clear that you can never write a novel about some abstract person. If you write a novel that would say that this person has fallen in love with that person, and you describe their emotions in general, the reader will somehow feel that it is a lie. Because there is no such thing as a person in general. Every person is completely different—and these differences are more important to literature than what is common between people.

So this is how I begin to speak about "storytelling," since the same thing is obviously true about the short story. A good story is not just a variation of another story. It has to be a variation of the human species—a variation of all the things that happen to us. It is not only that the things that happen to us are not exactly the same as the things that happen to our neighbors. Even the days of our own lives are not the same. Today is a little different from yesterday—and there is a good chance that tomorrow will be different from today. When you write a letter and you say, "The days pass one after the other, they are all like," it is nothing but a phrase. They are not at all alike and we all know this.

As a boy I often wondered, when I read stories—not fiction stories but history—why I was not satisfied. Here is a book of history which recounts so many things, and somehow I feel it is good, but it is not what I want. Because what I really wanted—and what I was not given as a clear account—was to know the *people* of the history. Not only to say that, on a certain day, 20,000 Poles went out to fight 20,000 Hungarians, and half of them were killed and a great number of them were wounded. I wanted to know these people, and history could not tell me their life stories—because it is not its duty to give the individuality of these armies and what happened to them and how they felt. And I began to feel that the reason why history was not satisfying to me was that it had no individuality. I couldn't find all these people's fingerprints—the spiritual fingerprints of who they were. When I read *War and Peace* as a young boy, I hoped

I would find the Napoleonic Wars, with all the soldiers' stories. But after a while it was clear to me that, although *War and Peace* was a very long novel—over a thousand pages—Tolstoy couldn't do this. He would have needed a half million pages to write about all these soldiers and all the people who fought and fell in the war. And he could not really explain their feelings and emotions. Literature cannot do this. Tolstoy understood that it would be enough for readers if he described some of the people who took part in this war, a few of the soldiers, and we would learn from them as much as we could. Because to get the address of one person is one thing, but to get the address of thousands of people is quite different.

I think of all those companies that send out advertisements to people. They get the addresses of half a million people and they let them know that their soap, or whatever they produce, is the best and they should buy it. They really don't need to know the individuality of all these people, they need their money, which they get. This is the same reason we don't like writers who write only for the sake of money. Of course writers all want to make some money and are very happy to get a check from their publishers. But once you sit down to write for money, you become like a company, and you do the same thing a company does. A company gets addresses and telephone numbers and doesn't care about anything else. But real writers care very much about their own individuality and about the individuality of other people.

When I began, as a young boy, to investigate literature in my own way, I came to a conclusion that, as it looked to me then, couldn't be true. But the longer I pondered it, the more I came to believe it was true. There are two basic topics in literature.

One basic topic is love—a love story. I asked myself why this is so. We do not only indulge in making love—we do business, we have banks, we build factories, we go to work, we do millions of things. So why should love be almost the only topic in literature? And I rebelled against it. I said: I am going to write a story that will have no love at all. It will not be a love story. It will be the story of how a man built up a little factory in a little village where I lived—or how a man decided to study and become an engineer and how he reached, or didn't reach, his goal. And I tried in my own way to conduct many experiments, and I also learned that many writers tried this. Because in my time, when I was a boy, the Russian Revolution was already a fact and many writers wanted to write the story of the Revolution. Why not? Here is a great revolution, a great sociological event, why not write about it? And of course the critics and the Stalinists said: Write about what happened in October!

There were people who wrote about it, but it was not real literature. What was the reason? The first reason is that literature cannot write about the masses. It can only write about a few people. In *War and Peace* only a few people are left in our memory—and we remember them. Some of the people that Tolstoy tried to describe did not come out as well as he wanted. This happened was when Tolstoy made them discuss the Russian situation of his time, like giving back the land to the peasants. All these topics in themselves could not become a real work of fiction. As soon as Tolstoy tried to talk about peasants—not only one peasant but millions of peasants—he could not really do it with literature. Sociology can do this in its own small way. Psychology can describe millions of people in terms of some psychological laws. But literature cannot do this. So I had to make peace with this and understand that we are limited in this respect. And since we cannot and will not succeed, maybe I should also do what other writers did. They wrote about a few people whom they knew best.

The second conclusion to which I came was more precarious, and many people would tell me that it was a mistake then and is still a mistake today. But my conclusion was that almost all talented people—no matter what kind of education they have been given, no matter what their background—all somehow think and brood about the so-called eternal questions. The eternal questions are the questions that many of us ask ourselves: Why was I born? Why must I die? Why am I here? What is the purpose of all these days, what is the purpose of all my struggles, and what is the purpose of all my disappointments? It is a kind of philosophical questioning and somehow literature is full of these questions.

People who never ask themselves these questions and who make peace with them, also think that life is as it is, that people are as they are, and that everything that happens to us is history. Since we cannot help it, let's ignore it. But real artists cannot ignore it. They keep on asking themselves the eternal questions. Many of the great writers came to religion, as happened with Tolstoy. After becoming a literary master—a great power and really a beacon of his time—he suddenly began, in his old age, to ask the questions that little children ask themselves. He could somehow not make peace with the fact that he was destined to live a few years and disappear forever. He kept asking himself: Is this why I am here in this world? And somehow it bothered him to such a degree that one day he decided he must become a real Christian and create his own version of Christianity. He began an argument with his family, with the Russian clergy, with nearly everyone, and began to say that *Anna Karenina* and *War and Peace* are not really such important works because they didn't deal with these topics.

Actually, he was mistaken. *Anna Karenina* and *War and Peace* deal very much with these topics—why we are born, why we must die, what is the purpose of everything. He did not write this as clearly as he wanted in his life's later years, but the questions were there. And the same thing can be said of Dostoevsky. Though he began as a revolutionary and a near-atheist, the longer he lived, the more he came to the basic eternal questions.

I would not say that all these things I am talking about now are the basis of literature, because literature is larger than this. Writers all bring with them specific information—and not about what is going on in Heaven or what will happen after death. They have never had and cannot have this kind of information. Writers are as blind about this as are other people. But they give us a little information, the fingerprints of human beings, and these fingerprints, though they may not be very important for Spinoza or Kant or Schopenhauer, are very important for readers—for all of us. Because just as we are different from everybody else, so everyone else is different from us, and we are eager to see these differences.

Where are the fingerprints of all these people who live today and who lived in the recent years?

Many people ask me what has happened to literature in our time and I ask myself the same question. I say to myself: the nineteenth century brought us geniuses like Tolstoy and Dostoevsky and Flaubert and Maupassant and Chekhov. But in the twentieth century, especially in the second half, writers began, for some reason, to go down rather than up. I ask myself: Why can't we have another Tolstoy or another Dostoevsky or another Flaubert or another Strindberg, whom I consider to be a great and wonderful writer. I answer myself that something has happened to writers in our time which should not have happened. They have forgotten their real mission. They have begun to think that they can really speak about the masses, that they can plan the future! We know that in our life we have moments of forgetfulness or amnesia. Sometimes you promise yourself that you are going to write a letter to a certain relative, maybe to your mother, and day after day after day passes, and you forget about it.* There are reasons for this forgetting and sometimes you are ashamed about it. You say: How could I have forgotten to write my beloved mother a letter? But somehow you forget because somewhere you think that there are more important things than writing to your mother. You become practical and pragmatic.

Modern literature has fallen into a state of amnesia because of all these revolutions—because of the great mass movements which are happening in our time. People like Karl Marx and Lenin, and also fascists like Hitler and Stalin, are telling people: you are not important, your mother is not important, the most important thing is the revolution, for millions of people to rebel. And this permeates our spirit to such a degree that our literature forgets to write its little letter to its old mother.

When I look at the literature of our time, I see that it reflects this kind of forgetfulness. They say about a professor of mathematics that he once undertook a long calculation and that it took him months to figure out. There was a bad mistake somewhere. Suddenly he discovered that he had forgotten that one plus one is two. And I think this is happening in literature and in many of the arts. We sometimes forget the main thing.

* Editor's note: Singer's story "A Letter to Mama" is about a man who puts off writing to his mother in Poland until decades pass and he feels that she has died. It was published in the *Forverts* on October 29, 1965. This may help place the writing of this essay in the same period.

Literature for Children and Adults

One of the biggest biological enigmas is the great gift—or the great burden—of emotions that Nature has bestowed upon people. No matter how impoverished we might be in all other areas, we are millionaires in emotions. People need not study emotions the way they study languages or sciences. What's more, all the intelligence we have accumulated over the centuries goes to serve these emotions, and sometimes to regulate them somewhat, so that in the mad impetus of our emotions, we don't inundate ourselves. In this area, the beggar is as rich as the king. Idiots are often as rich in emotions—and sometimes even more so—than geniuses. The human infant emerges from the womb more helpless than any other creature and remains so for a relatively long time, but it begins almost immediately to display fear, rage, an appetite for amusement, and many other emotions that have not been confirmed to date. Intellectual prodigies are rare, but when it comes to feelings, we are all prodigies.

The following essay appears in the archives in both Yiddish and English type-scripts with handwritten corrections. Singer published a similarly titled article in the *Forverts*, "Literatur far dervaksene un litertur far kinder" (Literature for Adults and Literature for Children, Nov. 30, 1969, section 2, page 11) under the name Yitskhok Bashevis, but this article—revisiting some of the ideas he pursues in other essays on literature—has little in common with this English-language essay. No other information has been found about the composition of this essay.

So prodigious and powerful are our feelings that almost from the beginning children must be taught how to suppress them. It's not an exaggeration to say that if people were to give in to their emotions for even one day—sometimes even for a minute—they would bring destruction down upon themselves and their loved ones. Even the so-called savages learn at an early age to curb and control their emotions. It is also true that if people were to lose all their emotions through some occurrence, they would be left as idiots even if they possessed the intelligence of Newtons and Einsteins. A person without feelings would be as dead as a computer.

It's remarkable how poor language is, particularly in words able to convey emotions. Even the restricted number of such words that do exist—such as joy, anxiety, happiness, satisfaction, peace of mind, unrest, ambition, love, hate, and so on—are so vague, ambiguous, and unspecific that they are practically meaningless. When we say about people that they are chopping wood, drinking water, eating bread, studying geometry, or that they are letter carriers, tailors, or farmers, we know much more about them than if we were to say that they are pleased, happy, unhappy, in love, astounded, insulted, impatient, loyal, proud, cheerful, or sad. We have to use many words—often hundreds or thousands—to describe a state of mind, and this often requires artistic talent.

Those who take an interest in literature and its methods know that the greatest masters refrained from calling emotions by name and instead described the circumstances that evoked these emotions in their countless variations. What's more, no words grow so stale and cliché-ridden with time as those that express emotions. "I regret," "I am pleased," "I am happy," "I look forward to," "sincere," "cordial," "devoted," "friendship," "greeting," "brotherly," "I hope," "I anticipate," and many other

words and phrases of this kind don't even reach the rank of cliché. Most of the banalities employed by bad poets, stage lyri-
cists, and politicians constitute words or expressions in this
category. When we say that a certain man is suffering, he might
as easily have cancer as have not received enough votes to become the president of a synagogue. It's the same with disappointment, ecstasy, irritation, longing, wishing, regret, love,
respect, esteem, satisfaction, or wonder. In his *Ethics*, Spinoza
tried to define the emotions—the affects—and in doing so
condemned nearly all of them as passions that dim the intellect
and serve as the major cause of human tragedy. But Spinoza
also acknowledged that emotions are just as necessary and
equally a part of God as reason.[1]

It is remarkable that children avoid these words as much as
possible. Ask children if they are happy, and they will answer
"yes," but at the same time they will view the person posing this
question with a kind of contempt for having asked it. Children
sense that this word lacks clear meaning unless you accompany
it with a number of concrete examples. When they talk among
themselves, they use nouns and verbs that require no additional
modifications. In our time, psychologists and psychoanalysts
have fashioned an impressive number of words to describe
human emotions and complexes, but some of these have already grown stilted, and others are so ambiguous that they have
no validity. One such word, for instance, is "guilt." It is used in
so many instances that it has lost all meaning.

Why aren't there enough words to convey our emotions?
How is it that the extensive psychiatric lexicography hasn't created a more precise vocabulary? The reason is that the emotions
are so specific—so dependent upon the individual character,
personality, time, place and circumstance—that no generaliza-
tion can describe them, and words are generalizations. Emotion

is a phantom that doesn't let itself be weighed, measured, counted or photographed.[2] Emotions are best depicted in situations, stories. Emotions, like the molecules of a protoplasm, come in complete systems, chains, or clusters. Most of them aren't expressed but suppressed. Despite all of modernity's efforts to divest itself of Adam and Eve's fig leaf and to put an end to shame, people today bear more shame than all the generations before them. They are ashamed of their suffering, and, more than anything, of their urge for the kind of happiness they know they can never attain. Most of all, they are ashamed of being ashamed.

Anyone who wants to write for children must remember that children are frequently no poorer in emotions than adults. Often, a child's emotions are stronger and even more complex, but the child is less inclined to let itself be duped by imprecise words and abstractions. You can speak to grownups about love in general and they will form the illusion that they know what you're talking about, but the child insists on immediately knowing who loves whom. Children want to hear stories because they instinctively know that life is made up of stories. Children know that every love is different and that each encounter between people represents a kind of truth that has never occurred before, nor will ever occur again. Unlike adults, who presuppose that every drama is melodrama and therefore demand many details and proofs to convince themselves that a story is true, children know that the human imagination is itself a part of truth if it contains action and suspense. The simple fact that a story is suspenseful is a sign to children that it contains life. Children are different from those jaded and skeptical readers or critics who believe that only boredom is realistic.

Because children are so eager for specifics, they love illustrations. For children, the illustration is a bonus rendering the story more specific. Every effort to provide young readers abstractions instead of concrete incidents, or symbols instead of events—or to expose them to illustrations that do not resemble the protagonists of the story—is doomed to failure. Children are prepared to give the author and artist a lot of credit so long as they don't denigrate this credit with sloppy daubs, absurdities, false logic, or inconsistent behavior. In other words, children demand from the storyteller all the traits literature should possess, without any of its defects.

In no other time has a lack of talent functioned with so many theories as in ours. The untalented writers of earlier days tried—within the limits of their capabilities—to fit themselves to the standards set by true talent. They made an effort to tell a story. If they were unable to be dramatic, they became melodramatic. If they couldn't describe emotion through images and situations, they filled the narrative with sentimentality. If they were unable to build solidly, they created weak or shaky structures. But they never had the chutzpah to say that what the masters had done was bad and that what they did was good. And yet the talentlessness of our time still tries to conceal its ineptitude with theories. Since it lacks the power to tell a story, it contends that the story is superfluous, old-fashioned, even harmful. What's important is the message—the symbol. When its psychology begins to sag, it substitutes sociology. When it lacks the power to describe love, it substitutes pornography. When the very essence of reality eludes it, it turns to pseudo-symbolism. All its arrogance stems from the fact that business is on the side of literary mass production. Publishers, printers, and bookbinders cannot wait for genes to combine such that talent is born. Our time has spawned a kind of journalism that supplies readers with novels based on political happenings and current gossip. Thank God, our children aren't so interested in politics, and even less in literary theories.

The arrogant mask behind which the talentlessness of our generation hides is the mask of "originality." Kafka, Joyce, and other such genuine creators, all of whom[3] placed their whole emphasis on originality, unwittingly opened wide the gates to a flood of fabricated originality. There has evolved a literature of tricks and gimmickry. These writers wantonly and systematically cripple and pervert the order of ideas and things, of image and action. They make do without consistent plot or lifelike characters. They maintain that dialogue no longer needs to fit those who are conducting it. Writers can arbitrarily put words into their characters' mouths that they, the writers, know will impress their readers with their pseudo-originality. Even correct syntax and punctuation are no longer required.

Every gimmick is acceptable so long as it is allegedly new. One writer brings Freud to New York, a second might bring Lord Byron or Pushkin to Chicago. The possibilities are endless. Why can't Spinoza be transported to our century, placed in a furnished apartment in Greenwich Village, and become involved in an affair with Emma Goldman? Why can't Lenin run for president of the United States against Nixon? The banality of our time wants to be super daring, radically different.[4] The banality of our time has studied literature, it has taken all kinds of courses in creativity. It knows all the literary fads, all the whims of the publishers, critics, theater managers, and film producers. The artistic impatience of our age wants to consciously trade love for pornography and to mask its impotence with a mechanical super potency. It wants to dictate artistic fashion for every season just as it does in the clothing industry. A fashion dictatorship in every kind of art is not some danger. It already exists. And chances are good that it will emanate not from Paris but from New York.

So successfully does such deception and chaos thrive in writing and in art for adults that efforts are being made to introduce these gimmicks and fads into literature and illustration for children. I have read children's books in which one word bears no relationship to another. They're already trying to suckle our children on writing lacking all plot and logic, and on illustrations that constitute one big mess. Sentences are being written for our children lacking subject, predicate, and object. A number of writers have banished punctuation from their children's books. I have read children's books full of hatred of parents and teachers. The idea is that this will prepare young readers for what will come later, that they have to be prepared for the idea that ugliness is beauty and coarseness is refinement. But based upon my own experience, I must say that our children don't allow themselves be to as easily hypnotized or duped by fashion, authority, or advertising as do adults. They often display more character than their parents. Children don't grow excited over fabricated originality. There exists within the child an independence that many adults have already lost. Due to the very fact that children are themselves new—fresh from the womb— they don't share such veneration for novelty and youth. Children don't care about keeping up with the times. They have an interest in history and a respect for things that happened long before them.

Children have no difficulty accepting the existence of God— of angels and devils. Children, you might say, have an instinctive sense for the supernatural. It's not easy for them to accept the notion that the universe evolved from an explosion, that creation was a physical or chemical accident. Children still believe in reward for good deeds, and punishment for evil. They have sympathy for the victims of crime rather than for criminals.[5] Children have no interest in literature that deals with collectives or masses. They know better than grownups that literature lacks the ability to describe masses. You can mention peoples, armies, or wars in a children's book, but merely as a background for a story about individual characters. Children hold no respect at all for what is average or lacking in character. They are bored by the antihero. They aren't interested in puzzling and tricky language. Children demand short sentences and a language that's precise. At play, children sometimes babble absurdities, but in a book they want the words and sentences to follow a logical order. Children don't want authors to write down to them. They want to look up both to the writer and to the book. When children read poetry, they want the verses to have rhyme and rhythm. They flatly reject the whole false Modernism both in literature and in art. As paradoxical as it may sound, children are to a high degree old-fashioned readers—not because they were raised this way, but because the so-called avant-garde art is so meager in plot and individuality—because it is so boring. Children often secretly read books written for adults, but never those that are tricky in style and don't tell a story.

The demagogues of all times have exerted great effort to draw children into their nets. Thousands of children's books were written about the greatness of Hitler and Stalin. The Soviets believed that children's books in Russia would help raise the kind of "new person" that communism planned to create—a person for whom the decisions of the Central Committee and the Politburo would take the place of religion. But the party leaders have been bitterly disappointed. Soviet literature for children hasn't given birth to a "new person." There still exists in Russia a deep longing for religion and even an inclination toward mysticism. Here in America, some try—through television, films, and books—to infuse children and adults with a kind of worldliness that glorifies murder, theft, robbery and rape.[6] They are trying to erase children's natural respect for their parents.[7] The aesthetic downhill slide of our time goes hand-in-hand with the tendency to invert all our ethical values. The writer of children's literature must be aware of these forces and must have the courage[8] to make a choice. No one is asking authors of children's books to assail their young readers with tedious messages. It's enough that writers be aware of the role they play in the rearing of future generations.

The sinister tolerance toward chaos and crime that pervades justice—particularly for the crimes and vandalism of youth—didn't evolve on its own. In all times there were forces seeking[9] to transform human culture into anti-culture. The Sodom described in the book of Genesis is not some legend but a part of reality. Whole cities, countries, and collectives can become corrupted. There are cultures whose conscious or subconscious goal is collective suicide. In such cultures, a child is from the very beginning raised to believe that order is disorder, good is evil, and beauty is ugliness. Not only little Sodom but whole empires have collapsed under such conditions.[10]

Ethics and aesthetics are more firmly bonded than it might appear. Chaos in literature goes together with chaos in many other areas. We live in a time when the division between the world and the underworld has grown dismally thin and it often seems to have vanished altogether. The judge and the criminal read the same bestsellers, attend the same plays, laugh at the same vulgar jokes, and often speak the same jargon.

In order to develop spiritually, children must be raised in terms of right and wrong, beauty and ugliness, "you may" and "you may not"[11]—of acts that are acceptable to the higher powers and those that are repugnant to the higher powers. Neither Marxism, nor Leninism, nor false liberalism possesses this spirit. Without a belief in higher powers,[12] no valid aesthetic can be created. The decline of literature and art in the second half of this century is closely tied to the fact that great numbers of people have ceased to believe in God and begun to believe in Stalins, Hitlers, and the other idols of our era.

I am glad to say that our children resist. The child's preference for what is genuine and just is becoming more and more a guide for weakened and perplexed adults. The child's instinct has proven stronger than all the doubts and illusions of the confused adult. It is not an exaggeration to say that the child is our only hope for returning to the[13] faith in an orderly universe.

Yiddish and Jewish Life

The Kabbalah and Modern Times

What can a modern person learn from the Kabbalah? My definition of such a person is someone who does not believe in any authority, who does not rely on old texts, and who is looking for the truth in a scientific manner. When such people come to the higher questions, they are skeptical. I could therefore call my lecture, "What can skeptics learn from the Kabbalah?" Has it any value for them today? Or is it only a part of the history of human faith and superstition?

I consider myself a skeptic as far as dogma and revelation are concerned, and I will therefore try to convey to you my own feelings about the Kabbalah. Even if my skepticism is a little different from that of others, I still believe that there are those among you who think and feel as I do.

I have had, as you perhaps know, a deeply religious education. To my father and grandfather, every word of the Bible, the Talmud, and the commentaries was God's word. But very early I began to see that many things that are ascribed to God are human-made. After all, my parents had acquired all their religious

No Yiddish original has been found for this essay and no entry matching this title or topic appears in any existing bibliography. Singer mentions giving a lecture with this title at the University of Michigan and Wayne College in an article published in the *Forverts* under the name Varshavski on March 2, 1965, grounding the essay in this period, and the Ransom Center also has an audio recording of the lecture, given at the 1976 Panarion Conference.

knowledge from books, and books are written by people. I saw how one law in the Bible became eighteen laws in the Mishnah, and seventy in the Gemara. I read about miracles that seemed, to me, completely unbelievable. Everything was founded on hearsay, on what one person said and another one wrote. I soon understood that one can seldom rely on the testimony of others. Some people suffer from hallucinations, others bear false witness. My own parents, who worshipped every Jewish book, contended that the books of other faiths were false. They themselves declared that one could not rely on old parchments and prophets if they happened to belong to another faith.

Long before I read David Hume and Immanuel Kant, I came to the conclusion that one could not prove the existence of God, the soul, free will, or other religious truths by logic. One could certainly not prove by logic that this or that person had had a revelation, or that God had told them exactly how to speak and what to do. In the commentaries of Rabbi Ibn Ezra, I found traces of biblical criticism. I found arguments for and against the principles of religion in such books as *The Guide for the Perplexed*, *The Kuzari*, *Beliefs and Opinions*, and *Duties of the Hearts*. Very early I had the opportunity—and the burning curiosity as well—to read Spinoza's *Ethics*, Kant's *Prolegomena*, and Hume's *Treatise on Human Understanding*. To this day, I consider David Hume the strongest and most sincere philosopher of all.

With so many statements of faith before me, my skepticism only grew. It was in this state of mind that I began to read books about the Kabbalah. Young as I was, I approached it with the feeling that I would not find the truth in it. On the contrary, I was convinced in advance that everything the kabbalists said was the product of a subjective point of view, and that no God or angel had been revealed to them. What drove me to read the philosophers and the kabbalists was the great mystery I saw around me. I stood in the evenings on the balcony of our apartment at 10 Krochmalna Street and looked at the sky. The moon wandered over the tin roofs and chimneys. The sky was alive with stars. I had read in a popular book of astronomy that some of the stars were larger than the Earth or even the Sun. Some of them were so far away that it took thousands or millions of years for their light to reach my eyes. On warm summer days, our balcony was visited by butterflies and other insects of all shapes and sizes. I had read that a housefly has thousands of eyes. All these creatures have stomachs, respiratory and reproductive organs. Each is made up of millions of molecules, and each molecule is a complicated construction of atoms. There had to be a plan behind all of this. I had read a Yiddish pamphlet on Darwin, but somehow his theory did not satisfy me. I was ready to admit that evolution had taken place, but behind this evolution there must have been powers with a purpose and a meaning.

It is not easy to find a kabbalistic book which clearly explains the point of view of the Kabbalah. In almost all of these books, the basic philosophy is obscured by too many references to Jewish laws and customs. Also, there are many systems in the Kabbalah itself, like the system of Rabbi Moshe of Cordova, or that of Rabbi Isaac Luria. The Kabbalah, like the Talmud, is a sea, and if one cannot swim in it, one sinks. But if one searches at length and with patience, a clear pattern begins to emerge.

This pattern reveals a thoroughly pantheistic system. Like Spinoza, the kabbalists believe that there is no basic difference between God and the world. The famous Baal Shem expressed it with the words, "God is the world and the world is God." But still, there is a difference between the pantheism of Spinoza and that of the Kabbalah. According to Spinoza, substance has existed always. There was no creation. Spinoza's God has neither will nor purpose, neither pity nor justice. Spinoza's God has no freedom in the sense that we mortals understand it. He is actually a prisoner of his own laws. When Spinoza says God, he means Nature. Spinoza's God has only two attributes that people can observe—extension and thought—and these are two sides of the same coin. Also, for Spinoza's God, might is right. From Spinoza's point of view, Genghis Khan, the Baal Shem, a tiger in the jungle, Gandhi, Hitler, and Stalin are all part of the Godhead, necessary manifestations of the infinite substance. There can really be no talk of good and evil, of reward and punishment. According to Spinoza's philosophy, the Holocaust wrought by Hitler in Europe was as inevitable as the eruption of a volcano.

In the Kabbalah, everything begins with God.

Before the world was created, the Kabbalah teaches us, only God existed, or as the kabbalists call him, *Ein Sof*, the Infinite. What God really is, no individual can fathom. His attributes began to reveal themselves only after God had begun his creation.

"Why did God create?" asks Rabbi Chaim Vital in his famous book *The Tree of Life*. His answer is that "creation is one of his attributes." God is, by his divine nature, a creator. Besides, how can there be a king without subjects? How can there be love without creatures to be loved? How can there be mercy without someone to receive it? Until God began to create, his attributes were merely potential, not actual. God's goodness demanded the existence of a world.

But how could God create a world if God himself filled infinite space, and, as the *Zohar* expresses it, there was no space empty of him? Rabbi Isaac Luria provided an answer: "God had to diminish himself." He had, in some part of his being, to extinguish his light and thereby create a vacuum, which is called *tsimtsum*. Naturally, such conceptions are anthropomorphic, since to give readers some understanding of the problem, the Kabbalah had to use human concepts. The Kabbalah describes God as a light which fills infinite space. In the middle of that light, a dark area appeared, which was a vacuum. Into this vacuum, God threw a beam of light which emanated from him and was part of him. In this action, God's attributes or *sefirot* became manifest. According to the Kabbalah, God has ten attributes which repeat themselves in all his works: the crown, wisdom, understanding, mercy, strength, beauty, eternity, majesty, fundamentality, and kingship. Yes, God's creation is a part of God, but diminished or attenuated to the point where God's glory could be perceived. According to the Kabbalah, God created four world systems—the world of emanation, the world of creation, the world of forms, and the world of deeds. The last of these worlds is the material world, or the universe. Indeed, the cosmos, with its myriads of galaxies and nebulae, is the lowest of God's system of worlds. At this stage, God's light has become so dim that it has turned into matter.

Since the purpose of creation is that God should be able to grant mercy to those who need it, it is clear that the further away a world is from God, the more it is in need of his goodness. When a father keeps his child close to him, that child is not hungry for a good word or a gift in the way a child is who is sent to a faraway country. According to the Kabbalah, the planet Earth is more remote from God than any other world. We who are here are exiles. We live in darkness and in the cold. God's mercy seldom reaches us. We have frequent moments of fear and doubt. Often we are not even sure whether we have a father. But just because we are so far away from the source of light, we are able to appreciate mercy when it reaches us.

The kabbalists believed that there is little free will in the higher spheres. Those near to God and his light *must* recognize him. Free choice is possible only where there is suffering and despair.

The planet on which we live is called by the kabbalists "the den of devils, the abyss of Satan." Here all the dark powers hold sway: Lilith, Shivta, Na'ama, Mahlat. All this darkness and evil is necessary for people to have the power of free choice, and for all their deeds and thoughts to be in a perpetual balance between right and wrong. But just because of this condition, God can manifest more creativity and more mercy here than in other spheres. Our world is a stage teeming with villains who persecute the few good characters and try to destroy them. But somehow the good fights and struggles unceasingly. Life on Earth is a play with innumerable acts, with infinite theses, antitheses, and syntheses. In a sense, the Kabbalah paints a Hegelian picture, or even a Marxist one. However, instead of class struggles, the Kabbalah sees an endless struggle between light and darkness.

The question asked of all pantheistic systems is, "Where does evil come from?" According to the Kabbalah, the devil has no positive substance. Evil is only a lack of goodness, just as darkness is a lack of light. When God diminished himself and created a vacuum, that very vacuum became evil. However, the absence of God's light varies. In the higher spheres there is little darkness. Those who are near God are flooded with his radiance. But the farther away from God, the darker it becomes, the sadder, the emptier, and all of this taken together adds up to faithlessness, hate, envy, wickedness, and materialism. There is not enough of the divine light to point the way. For every truth, we must fight and pay a high price. To learn that certain mushrooms are poisonous, we had to eat the mushrooms and die from eating them. To discover that certain deeds lead to destruction, we had to commit these deeds and be punished. Yes, the Kabbalah also believes in evolution, but this is not an evolution without direction.

Spinoza's God is static. He is always the same. He is an infinite machine. Nothing can be added to him, nothing can be taken away. In God, there can be no revolution, even evolution is impossible, because everything is predetermined. In contrast, the God of the Kabbalah is creative and, in a sense, dependent on his creatures. He himself is free, and he delegates freedom to his creatures, because without freedom creation is impossible. God himself doesn't build houses, write books, paint pictures on canvas, or engage in any of the other lesser activities destined for his creatures. In a deep sense, creation is, according to the Kabbalah, a divine experiment. The giver of freedom cannot, after the granting of such freedom, be an absolute ruler. Once granted, freedom can always be used for good or for evil. The sinner disappoints God and does harm to his experiment. If people succeed, the whole of creation is a success. One might say that humans are the weakest link in God's chain, and we know that a chain is only as strong as its weakest link. If people are able to overcome Satan, they give meaning to the whole of creation.

The Kabbalah continually emphasizes that everything a person does on Earth influences the upper spheres. Angels, seraphim, and cherubim are uplifted by people's virtuous actions. On the other hand, each transgression creates sadness on high. When people do evil, they cause God to suffer, because the evil deeds mean that God's creation is a failure. The Midrash tells us that before God created people, he asked the advice of the angels, and many of them warned him that by creating humans, he was risking, as it were, his divine career. The angels contended that humanity might shame God's creative talent, his genius. But God didn't listen to the angels. He risked everything to create humankind, hoping that in the long run people would learn the truth.

Since the Kabbalah made the Godhead a dynamic power and gave it, so to speak, human qualities, it could not leave out love and sex. Spinoza compares those who love to the insane. To him each passion is a weakness, an affect. Even pity and a sense of justice are no more than emotions, which reason must overcome. But the God of the Kabbalah is emotional. According to the Kabbalah, there are godly emotions just as there are human ones. Among God's attributes there is mercy and beauty, which are emotional attributes. The principle of the masculine and the feminine exists in all worlds.

Even God possesses a feminine aspect, which is called the *Shekhinah*. God did not create the world by himself. He needed a divine female to give birth to creation. Different kabbalists had different approaches to the meaning of the *Shekhinah*, which had been mentioned even in the Talmud. There it is said that when creation goes according to divine plan, God and the *Shekhinah* come closer together. Conversely, sin and evil keep God and the *Shekhinah* apart. One might compare them to loving parents who feel renewed love for each other when their children are good. According to the Talmud and the Kabbalah, the *Shekhinah* tries to defend people before the throne of the Lord and to intercede on their behalf. When the Jews sinned and the Second Temple was destroyed, God forsook the *Shekhinah*, and full union could not take place again until the coming of the Messiah.

Just as God has his *Shekhinah*, so all the heavenly hosts have their feminine counterparts. In the celestial mansions, unions and copulations take place. Jacob continues to copulate with Rachel, Leah, Bilhah, and Zilpah. Some of the kabbalistic books are full of tales about divine eroticism. Since they are all nearer to God and his light, these unions and copulations are of a higher nature than their counterparts on Earth. Love on Earth is never pure. Love on Earth has its pitfalls, its crises. Here love is often marred by jealousy and cruelty, treachery and falsehood. Here copulation can be not only a virtue, but also a fatal sin. Here souls and bodies make all kinds of mistakes, and are capable of falling into the abyss of lechery and abomination. But just because love on Earth is so dangerous, each successful union is a joy and a triumph to God and to his divine host. Union on Earth brings about union in the spheres. A great and holy love on Earth brings the males and females in all the other palaces closer together.

Many critics of the Kabbalah, such as Rabbi Aryeh de Modena and Rabbi Jacob Emden, accused the kabbalists of obscenity. They decried some passages of the Kabbalah as pornography. It is true that the Kabbalah can be explained perversely, as was done by the disciples of the false messiah Sabbatai Zevi, and later by the followers of the impostor Jacob Frank. The Frankists went so far as to organize kabbalist orgies. Any law can be distorted. It is true that there are passages in the Kabbalah that look like descriptions of sexual perversions, but perversion itself is, according to the Kabbalah, a caricature of something which has a higher purpose in the divine order. Humanity's chief mission is correction. The kabbalists tell us that in certain processes of creation, sacred sparks fell into the unholy host, and that the saints must save these holy sparks from the lower depths and bring them back to their sacred origin. A great deal can be said about this part of the Kabbalah. Its real sense is that here on Earth, good and evil are so fused that it is difficult even for the wise to know where one ends and the other begins. Even saints have their selfishness. As long as the soul is imprisoned in the body, it shares the body's materialistic tendencies, but it is our duty to learn how to distinguish between the pure and the impure. In certain cases, a descent is necessary for an ascent. So God bade the prophet Hosea to marry a harlot in order that their union might serve as a symbol of God's relation to Israel. More than any idealistic philosophy, the Kabbalah understood that people could not ignore their bodies, its needs and desires.

The *Zohar* and the other kabbalistic books put a lot of weight on the biblical statement that humans were created in God's image. True, humanity is flesh and blood, poor in knowledge, but it is still a miniature of the Godhead, and one can learn from humanity what God is. And since the animals also resemble people, they too are in God's image. Both the Bible and the Talmud speak of sacred animals in Heaven. Everything on Earth has a divine counterpart. There are divine eyes, ears, a divine brain, divine hands and feet, divine genitals. Each passion below is modeled after a passion above. There, as here, monogamy and polygamy exist. There, as here, exists the principle of homosexuality. We are not just a minor planet in the Milky Way, as modern astronomy tells us. The kingdom of the Earth is a portrait of the kingdom of Heaven. Our microcosm reflects the macrocosm.

Although, according to the Kabbalah, evil is only the absence of good, this negative power also has its forms. Evil is not merely chaos. The powers of evil have a certain temporary independence. If God's experiment should fail, Satan and his unholy hosts may take dominion. Darkness is not less ingenious than light. The powers of Asmodeus and Armilus try with all their cunning to make evil permanent and to bring about God's downfall. They make an effort to bring disharmony into love, to infuse every good deed with hypocrisy, to create jealousy, hatred, arguments, calumny, treachery, cruelty. The Kabbalah gives many epithets to the powers of evil—insolent dogs, chaff of the grain, venom of the snake. Many scholars have pointed out the mutual influences between the kabbalists and the Gnostics. There are many systems in the Kabbalah, and a great many variations. Hasidism is, in fact, only a continuation of the Kabbalah of Rabbi Isaac Luria.

Since the kabbalists were Jews, and since they based the Kabbalah on the Bible, the Talmud, and the Midrash, they naturally regarded the Jews as the essence of humankind, and hence the very purpose of creation. The Jew, the Torah, and God are all identical, the *Zohar* tells us. The Kabbalah teaches that God created the world with the letters of the Torah. With the aid of numbers and word combinations, the kabbalists tried to make it seem as if all of their ideas were inherent in the Torah. The greatness of the Jew reflects the divine greatness. And the tragedy of the Jew is a reflection of the divine tragedy. The redemption of the Jew, the coming of the Messiah, will be a redemption for all creation. Nowhere is the love of Jewishness as great as in the *Zohar*, which was supposed to have been written by Rabbi Shimon bar Yohai, but was actually compiled by Rabbi Moshe de León in Spain in the thirteenth century. The love of the Jew, as it is expressed in the *Zohar*, is not chauvinistic. The Jew, as seen by the *Zohar*, symbolizes the powers of goodness.

And now I come to the main theme: What can the Kabbalah give to people today, to the skeptics who refuse to rely on old parchments, revelations, and miracles? What does the Kabbalah offer me and others like me?

My answer is that, in a wonderful way, the Kabbalah contains the best of all philosophical systems, all mystical teachings, and all religions. The God of the Kabbalah is identical with the world, but he is not mechanical. In the Kabbalah one can find the best of Plato, Aristotle, Plotinus, Spinoza, and even such philosophers as Leibniz, Hegel, Schopenhauer, and Nietzsche. The God of the Kabbalah is spirit, but also matter. He is good, but he also has to make a place for evil. He is dynamic and creative. He has not exhausted and will never exhaust his divine possibilities. His creatures are not mere toys fashioned for his pleasure, but active assistants in a divine project based on freedom and free initiative. In a sense, the God of the Kabbalah is tragic, as are all creators who can never be sure of whether or not they will have the full cooperation of their assistants. The God of the Kabbalah is actually a person infinitely magnified—a person with human desires, human fantasies, and human complexes. There is in the Kabbalah the expression *Adam Kadmon*, primordial man, who is actually the image of God. The Kabbalah tell us, "If you want to know what God is, learn what you are." It especially dwells on the human desire to create. Through our creative powers we fathom creation. Our human passions reflect the divine desires. Our yearning for happiness tells us what the Godhead is striving for. I do not insult the Kabbalah when I say that it also contains those verities which the pagans once knew, those living truths and joys which modern humanity has forgotten, and which it must one day recall.

This doesn't mean that the kabbalists were eclectics. They simply thought through all religious and philosophical possibilities, and made them parts of one great pattern.

The Kabbalah is not a closed system, like Spinoza's. It leaves open many possibilities for religious thinkers and mystics. The Kabbalah is not incongruous with modern science. Its belief that everything is an emanation of God's light accords with Einstein's law that mass is basically energy. Its emphasis on love and sex agrees with Freudian theory. Its assertion that the Earth is the worst of all the worlds is analogous to the pessimistic view of Schopenhauer. Its belief that our creative possibilities are at their greatest when we are at the bottom of the abyss agrees in a remarkable way with artistic experience. The Kabbalah is actually an artist's philosophy. I don't know of a single system that does not find its expression, and illumination, in the Kabbalah. Even Darwin and Malthus fit into its framework.

Since the purpose of creation is to develop God's powers and bring about divine bliss, the kabbalists were in their own fashion hedonists. For the Kabbalah, all of creation is one huge laboratory of happiness.

The Kabbalah emphasizes many times that because of our limitations we cannot understand things higher than ourselves. All of our words and ideas about God and the higher spheres are no more than subjective intimations. The way to truth, says the Kabbalah, is through moral and aesthetic exaltation, through the correction of mistakes, through prayer, charity, learning, and good deeds. Love and sex are also means by which people can uplift themselves. The Kabbalah, like its God, is rich in possibilities. At times I have the feeling that the Kabbalah has not yet been discovered. It is the truth of the future. It contains imaginative treasures of which we are still unaware.

The picture that I have painted of the Kabbalah expresses not only what I have learned, but also what I am myself, my personality, my ideas, and my work. Such is the Kabbalah, that every soul sees it in a personal light.

In my sketch of the Kabbalah, I have also portrayed my own soul, and given form to my own philosophy of art and being.

The Ten Commandments
and Modern Critics

What would happen if Moses were alive today and issued the Ten Commandments not on Mount Sinai with thunder and lightning, but in the form of a booklet or a brochure? How would he be received by the critics? The following are a few of the possibilities.

The first critic, whom I will label the Aesthete:

Mr. Moses's booklet, actually a proclamation (or leaflet), is difficult to categorize. It isn't fiction in the usual sense of the word, nor is it a work of science. Perhaps it could best be labeled a religious tract—still, there is little of religion in it. Mr. Moses speaks of God, but does it in such vague fashion that it is generally difficult to determine his meaning. Perhaps one could describe it as a kind of ethical programme composed by one who

This satirical piece first appeared in Yiddish under the name Varshavski in the *Forverts* as "Di tsen gebot un di moderne kritiker" (The Ten Commandments and Modern Critics, Feb. 14, 1965). It appeared in English translation in the July 1965 issue of *Cavalier Magazine*. Singer's personal essays on the nature of divinity reflect on the importance of the Ten Commandments, whereas these critiques, while exaggerated, point to questions around their social relevance.

hasn't an inkling of the history of ethics nor of its development and philosophy.

Mr. Moses is a naïve moralist, indeed. His style is bone dry, primitive and laconic. He speaks, allegedly, in the name of some God, but nowhere does he offer us proof of this God's identity or existence.

It would be altogether a waste of time to review this primitive tract if it hadn't become an instant best seller. Is this an indication that the public is sated with long-winded books and even extensive articles and yearns to read only single-paged proclamations? Or is it fascinated by the supposed objectivity of the programme?

That such a rudimentary sheet of paper could so impress millions upon millions of readers is a clear indictment of how low the taste of the reading public has sunk in our time. The astonishing success of the *Ten Commandments* is a reproof and a protest against all of modern literature. It is as if the mob were to cry out, "We want no fantasy, no knowledge, no philosophy, only the most basic words that any ten-year-old can understand, or even write." Just who is hiding behind the pen name of Moses? Maybe it actually is a child? Or is the whole thing a kind of literary spoof?

However it may be, the *Ten Commandments* has, overnight, become the hottest literary item in the world. The question remains—what can one read afterwards? There remain only the masterpieces printed on the backs of cereal boxes. . . .

A communist critic:

The astounding popularity of the *Ten Commandments* is, to my mind, no mere accident. It is directly linked to the disintegration of the capitalist order and the downfall of the so-called democracies. Mr. Moses would have us believe that he is un-aware of such things as the class struggle, racial struggle, ideologies, and political parties.

Like every capitalistic ethicist, he completely ignores the history of the working class, its struggle for a place in the sun, its fight against imperialism. He simply states, "Thou shalt not murder." But whom does he define by that commandment? Does he imply that the oppressed masses in the Congo must not stand up to their Belgian oppressors? Is he opposed to every kind of revolution? Does Mr. Moses not know, or is he simply feigning ignorance of the bloody struggle of the world proletariat for existence?

And the other commandments fall into the same category. For instance, "Thou shalt not steal." One may not steal, but one may exploit workers. Were Rockefeller, Ford, and Morgan not thieves?

Frankly reactionary is the commandment, "Thou shalt not covet thy neighbor's . . . wife . . . his ox, nor his ass. . . ." This commandment legitimates the curse of private property and it is likely the reason why the *Ten Commandments* has been received so warmly by the imperialists.

Behind all these "commandments" lies a well-masked glorification of capitalism and all its flaws. The *Ten Commandments* is the final death rattle of a system rotted through and through. Following the writings of Marx and Lenin, the *Ten Commandments* and its success are nothing more than a specimen of exotica and a symptom that capitalism has cast off its mask of respectability and reverted to the very most primitive form of propaganda and literary larceny. The *Ten Commandments* are commandments of reaction, imperialism, and neofascism. . . .

The critic who is a psychologist:

That Mr. Moses is an inept writer is incontrovertible. His "commandments" stem from a mind that demonstrates neither self-criticism, nor insight into the recesses of the human soul. His "Thou shalt not commit adultery," for instance, is, from the psychological standpoint, sheer nonsense. Can one command the human heart not to lust? Did Mr. Moses never read *Anna Karenina*, or *Madame Bovary*, not to speak of *Lady Chatterley's Lover* and other such works?

The commandment that shocks the reviewer most of all, however, is, "Honor thy father and thy mother. . . ." Any babe in the cradle these days knows that the parents are responsible for most of their children's complexes. The whole science of psychoanalysis rests on the Oedipus and Electra Complexes. Suppressed hatred of parents is the source of innumerable neuroses. But Mr. Moses has apparently never heard of Sigmund Freud. He proposes absolute respect of parents.

How such a mess of psychological illiteracy could have achieved such popularity in our time is truly an enigma. It is a manifestation of the resistance posed in our neurotic era against psychoanalysis and against all psychology in general. The *Ten Commandments* is a gauntlet flung in the face of modern psychology, a denial of every effort to enlighten man's psyche or conduct.

The enormous success of the *Ten Commandments* emphasizes the present generation's resistance to any intellectual exertion. I would say that Mr. Moses is an anti-intellectual, or perhaps simply a beatnik with everything a beatnik represents. The *Ten Commandments* are the commandments *of* a beatnik *for* beatniks. They will be forgotten along with the beatniks.

A critic who splits hairs:

I go on record that Mr. Moses is not half as simple as he tries to appear in his *Ten Commandments*. I see these commandments as a stroke of subtle sarcasm that can be approached and understood only on that basis. The *Ten Commandments* attempt to say, "This is the way the world would be if everyone took seriously the various religions and their spokesmen." Mr. Moses is, at most, an atheist, or, at least, an agnostic.

The fact that the public takes these "commandments" seriously is not Mr. Moses's fault. It isn't the first time the masses have taken earnestly works written tongue in cheek. Mr. Moses, undoubtedly, nurses a low opinion of the average reader's taste these days, and it must be admitted that his estimate is not far off. The *Ten Commandments* will go down in the annals of world literature as the very cleverest parody and satire of the twentieth century.

A critic who is a cultural historian:

All its other defects aside, the *Ten Commandments* is a work of plagiarism. Mr. Moses has copied word for word from the laws of Hammurabi, who lived 4,000 years ago. Some of Mr. Moses's "commandments" have been found among the papyri in Egypt. . . .

The whole brochure contains not one fresh idea, no solitary statement to inspire one's thinking. The "commandments" are all ambiguous and have factually no value in light of humanity's experience in the past few thousand years. It isn't inconclusive that Mr. Moses discovered these "commandments" carved on some rock or clay tablet, and copied them down letter for letter.

The success of these "commandments" is, to this reviewer, an indication that we are experiencing an intellectual regression to the Ice Age or, perhaps, even the Stone Age. From that standpoint, the success of the *Ten Commandments* is a sad phenomenon.

A critic who is an antisemite:

If any of our readers still harbor doubts about the Protocols of Zion and the Jewish plot to conquer the world, the *Ten Commandments* will convince them once and for all. Mr. Moses is a Jew and the God of whom he speaks is a Jewish God. He commands, ". . . the Sabbath day . . . keep it holy." He recalls that the Jews were brought out of the land of Egypt.

The "commandments" themselves are the strongest possible indication of Jewish degeneracy and perversion. If murder is a sin, then all the national heroes of every race throughout history have been criminals. If murder and adultery are crimes, then the whole history of the world is a history of crime. And all of world literature, from Homer to Genet, is a literature of the underworld.

"Thou shalt have no gods before me. Thou shalt not make unto thee a graven image . . ." is a denial of the history of art throughout the ages, beginning with the primitive idols up to the very latest art. Yahweh, along with his people, wants to monopolize everything and leave nothing to the Aryans. No antisemitic propaganda could better bare the soul of the Jews and their lust for world domination than these very ten "commandments" that are more properly a ten-point guideline in the Jew's masterplan to take over the world, enslave its peoples, its cultures, all of modern civilization.

The success of the *Ten Commandments* shows how far Jews have advanced their devilish plan. We do not exaggerate when we state that there remain but two works from which the world must choose its future: Hitler's *Mein Kampf* and Moses's *Ten Commandments*. If the world chooses suicide, Moses the Jew has provided a perfect blueprint. . . .

A critic from a Jewish magazine:

Despite the fact that the name Moses has a Jewish ring to it (a relative of Robert Moses?), we believe that the author of these "commandments" is not really a Jew. It may even be the pen name of an antisemite. The blurb mentions that Moses was brought up by an Egyptian princess. Is it possible that this so-called Moses is really an Arab from Nasser's camp? Our suspicions are founded on the following facts:

1. The entire style of the *Ten Commandments* is un-Jewish. It is completely lacking in Jewish warmth—what our enemies call "schmaltz." The literary style of the *Ten Commandments* is bone dry and has the military curtness of a general's order or of sentences from Mr. Goldwater's diatribes.
2. Why did Mr. Moses single out the Jews to heed his commandments not to steal, kill, or commit adultery? Was this a sly implication that we are particularly lacking in moral virtues while the others are a flock of holy lambs?
3. Not a single Jewish leader or organization is mentioned in these "commandments." As a matter of fact, Mr. Moses completely ignores the Jewish question and the problem of antisemitism. These and other factors arouse our suspicion that Mr. Moses is on the payroll of enemies of world Jewry. It is a documented fact that

since the "commandments" were published, world antisemitism has risen 3 and 3/4 per cent.

These "commandments" are a godsend to Mr. Toynbee & Company. We believe that the Anti-Defamation League should launch an immediate investigation into this anti-Jewish smear which is concealed behind middle-class morality and Jewish chauvinism.

A critic of a labor newspaper:

While organized labor struggles with conservative big business for a four-day work week, Mr. Moses urges the working classes to toil six days and rest only on the Sabbath. We strongly recommend that our brothers in organized labor refute this swan song of NAM reaction.

A gossip columnist:

It's common talk around Broadway that the holier-than-thou Mr. Moses, of the best-selling *Ten Commandments*, is leaving his wife, Zipporah, home in the tent these nights to cavort with his Ethiopian cutie. . . . The playboy's sister, Miriam, is so upset that she has broken out in a rash all over her body. . . . The Hip Set also hears that Moses is grooming his brother, Aaron, for the priesthood. . . .

The critic for a women's magazine:

Mr. Moses's equation of a woman with an ox and an ass is an insult to the entire female sex. He generally seems to consider women to be the property of men. We hope that our readers will unanimously reject this anachronism. . . .

The critic from a daily:

All other faults aside, Mr. Moses is negative throughout. Of the ten "commandments," six begin with: "Thou shalt not. . . ." Mr. Moses completely lacks a positive approach to humanity and its problems. Mr. Moses tells us quite definitely what not to do. But what are we to do? About that, Moses remains silent.

A critic from a small-town newspaper:

So far as my understanding of the *Ten Commandments* extends, they are designed to be carried out, not to simply serve as a literary essay, and I must say, from that standpoint, they are quite okay. If humanity would literally adhere to them, the world would become a paradise. But Mr. Moses is naive if he expects the world to take his commandments seriously. They will be read and forgotten, unless Hollywood decides to make them into a movie. . . .

The Spirit of Judaism

Before me lie dozens of photographs of religious Jews in the Williamsburg section of New York.[1] I see fur-edged rabbinical hats, long gaberdines, big beards, sidelocks, women in wigs and in bonnets that were already obsolete even in my youth in Warsaw. I know that thousands of Jews and non-Jews who see these people want to know: What does this signify? Are they all rabbis? Does it say anywhere in the Torah or Talmud that Jews must dress this way? Do they belong to some special Jewish sect? Neither the Reform, the Conservative, nor even those

This essay was first published in English as "The Extreme Jews" in *Harper's* in April 1967, and reflects an attempt to offer cultural context for Hasidic Jews in Williamsburg. It was later adapted into an introduction to Ira Moskowitz's collection of paintings, drawings, and etchings, *The Hasidim* (1973). The published Yiddish version appeared as two articles in the *Forverts* under two pseudonyms—the first as "Berd, peyes, un lange szhupitses" (Beards, Sidelocks, and Long Gaberdines, Nov. 30, 1966, pages 2 and 5), signed Yitskhok Varshavski, and the second as "A minderheyt vos hot geleygt di merhayt in kheyrm" (A Minority That's Excommunicated the Majority, Dec. 5, 1966, page 2), signed D. Segal. This is a prime example of how Singer published under different pseudonyms in Yiddish, but saw all his work as potential material to be translated and published under his known identity in major English-language magazines. This essay, almost more than any other, also shows the extent to which he understood the mindset of extremist Jews, among whom were his own parents and younger brother, and tried to explain their individuality without judging their lifestyle. Singer was himself considered an apostate by the Jews he describes, yet he understood the internal logic of their customs in broader historical, cultural, and spiritual terms.

Jews who attend Modern Orthodox services dress this way—so to what group do these people belong? And what is their reason for wearing clothes that make them so conspicuous?

It is even more astonishing to see Jews dressed this way driving trucks, carrying packages, or delivering goods. Among them are businessmen and workers. Since that is so, what reason is there for their rabbinical garb?

I was often puzzled too when I saw pictures of Gandhi wrapped in a sheet. Similarly, the world was amazed nearly a century ago when Tolstoy suddenly donned a Russian peasant's smock. Why did he do this? Many people in and out of Russia accused him of exhibitionism or simply of publicizing himself, though they should have known better. No matter what he did, he could not have made himself more famous than he already was.

Well then, what about the hippies in New York and in all the European cities who seem to have responded simultaneously to some silent command to grow long hair and beards, to neglect their clothes, and to associate with others as unkempt as themselves? Is this nothing more than a fad, or does such attire disguise some idea?

People seldom realize that a style of dress, of hair, and of every kind of external nonconformity represents a sort of language, albeit frequently vague and unintelligible. So far, no one has compiled a dictionary of these "languages," nor researched their grammar and syntax. Nevertheless, they are forms of expression. Long hair, beards, mustaches express meanings that short hair and clean-shaven upper lips and chins simply do not. A long garment "speaks" differently to us than does a short one. Languages themselves would have no significance if objects did not possess a speech of their own. World literature would be meaningless if the human spirit did not try to express itself in the most divergent possible ways. We are curious to see celebrities because their faces, their manners, their gestures, and their garments say things we cannot glean from their words and deeds alone. Gandhi becomes much more understandable to us when we see his face and mode of dress. Tolstoy somehow would not seem the same without his patriarchal beard. We cannot imagine him looking like Lord Byron, nor Dostoevsky resembling Kaiser Wilhelm. It would somehow seem inappropriate. Bare souls undoubtedly exist somewhere, but the souls with which we are familiar have wrapped themselves in bodies, in clothes, and in manners.

Women tend to be more sensitive to these "languages" and often place more emphasis on such things as clothes, hairdos, and jewelry. A man will seldom criticize another man's choice of suit or tie, but a woman will accurately analyze another's outfit and gather meaning from the way she dresses and fixes her hair. Homosexuals often dress exotically not only to facilitate recognition among themselves but out of a strong compulsion to express their personalities. Even people for whom it would be prudent to be inconspicuous, such as criminals, often dress in an identifiable fashion. The Russian revolutionists of the nineteenth century all had good reason to remain anonymous. Yet many of them let their hair grow long and wore wide-brimmed hats and red or black shirts with sashes and tassels. Today, the American radical frequently dresses somewhat differently than the conservative.

Besides expressing the human spirit, clothes and hairstyles also hold a key to self-discipline. A priest may occasionally be tempted to ride a carousel and eat an ice-cream cone, but he is not likely to do this while wearing his priestly garb. His very costume dictates that he conduct himself with dignity. A rabbi in a long cloak, a beard, and sidelocks is not likely to dally with a girl on a street corner. Tolstoy—by donning the peasant smock—forever precluded his attendance at the elaborate balls of the aristocracy that he described so well in his novels. Gandhi's attire kept him from becoming a man of the world. Clothes guard a person just as words do. Even if a nun got the urge to attend a nightclub, her habit would keep her from fulfilling this whim. Religious people of all times were aware of the weakness inherent in human nature. They knew that people are often more ashamed before their fellow human beings than before God. People ready to betray the loftiest principle will still take pains not to appear laughable or make themselves objects of other people's anger and scorn.

When Jews were driven from their land, they knew the peril that threatened their future existence—the necessity of mixing with strangers. No exiled people has lasted as a group for more than a generation or two. But Jews were determined to endure many generations of exile if necessary, to remain true to their God, to the Torah, and to their native land, even though it lay in ruins and was occupied by strangers. It was an undertaking without counterpart in the history of humankind. It could only be effected thanks to a mighty discipline and a colossal mysticism of upbringing and education. The basis of this discipline was the total estrangement from the peoples among whom the Jews would dwell—not a physical estrangement but a spiritual one. True, Jews were forced to do business with non-Jews and often to work for them. But that was the extent of their association. Jews had to erect a spiritual ghetto around themselves that was immeasurably more isolated and impregnable than the physical ghettos to which they were later confined. To the Jews, the A to Z of their religion was the law of the Torah, as written in Leviticus 18:3, "After the doings of the land of Egypt, wherein ye dwelt, shall ye not do: and after the doings of the land of Canaan, whither I bring you, shall ye not do: neither shall ye walk in their ordinances."

If non-Jews wore a short coat, Jews would wear a long one. If their hats were round, Jewish hats would be pointed. According to the Talmud, the book of Jewish religious law, Jews dared not even tie their shoelaces in the same way as their non-Jewish neighbors. These laws were established not out of enmity toward others, but rather as a reminder for Jews to adhere to certain conditions if they wanted to retain their identity for hundreds if not thousands of years. True, they sometimes copied the fashions of their neighbors, but in all instances they lent their own touches to them.

Advocates of the Jewish Enlightenment, who wanted Jews to take off their gaberdines and become Europeans, often mocked the rigors that the rabbis had imposed upon Jews through the generations. But all these laws and rigors were intended as shackles to curb Jews from mixing with others. Assimilation is a natural process. A minority always seeks to fit itself into the majority. The weak will inevitably fashion themselves after the strong. The temptations were tremendous. Often the people among whom the Jews lived forced them to integrate. Romantic unions between Jews and non-Jews were unavoidable. For hundreds and thousands of years, Jews forced themselves to go against human nature.

The form of dress they adopted made this integration more difficult. They instinctively altered the language of their host nation so that it became their own dialect and seemed alien and comical to their neighbors. They shaved their daughter's hair and themselves grew beards and sidelocks that labeled them as Jews even from a distance.

History shows that the segregation between non-Jew and Jew was not uniform through the ages. It was less pronounced in the Arab lands than in the Christian, and even there, variations existed in different times and in different places. Italian and Spanish Jews spoke the native languages among themselves and had close relations with the local inhabitants. The Jews of France, Germany, and Eastern Europe were the most isolated from the native populations. It is almost a truism that wherever segregation was least severe, assimilation was the strongest. It was axiomatic among Jews that once any of them made the slightest move to adjust their ways to those of the non-Jews, those individuals stood poised on the threshold of conversion. And Jews preferred to lose such people completely than to retain them in their camp and chance their infecting other Jews with their ideas. The community boasted but one weapon: excommunication.

By cutting away from the community anyone who broke the rules of spiritual segregation, the Jew practiced a kind of selection which retained in the community only its most devout members. For centuries, Jews had but one choice—either bear all the burdens of their faith or go over completely to the religion of the majority. Assimilation in today's sense of the word was nonexistent. It only came about through the emancipation of Jews after the Napoleonic Wars.

The Emancipation created a new type of Jew, one who could renounce the laws of religion yet remain a Jew—or at least not go all the way toward conversion. Such so-called worldly Jews were a riddle both to themselves and to the Christian world. Since they disobeyed the laws of their religion, what constituted their allegiance to their faith? Some people of this kind called themselves national Jews. Their Jewishness consisted of belonging to a group, or of speaking Yiddish or Hebrew. These modern Jews created Zionism and waged a struggle against antisemitism. Their kind includes many who claim that even if they wanted to assimilate, they would not be allowed to do so. Thus the worldly Jews who live outside of Israel belong to a

group that has no land and often no language of its own, but
share common interests, character, and personality. The modern Jew's identity may not be defined in any dictionary, but it
exists nevertheless.

Religious Jews, the pious ones, do not believe in the national Jews or in their future. To them, Jews without religion
are what they are to many non-Jews—an enigma, a mass of
contradictions, a paradox. If the pious Jews of former times
had to exert every effort to segregate themselves from non-
Jews, today's pious Jews must redouble these efforts to remain
apart not so much from their neighbors as from the great number of nonreligious Jews, or those who have tried to reform
Jewishness. To the very pious Jews of Williamsburg, those Jews
who are communists, freethinking Zionists, or members of
Reform or Conservative congregations are all heretics and can-
didates for assimilation and mixed marriage. And they place in
this same category Jews in Israel who either don't practice Jewishness or try to reform it there. Since danger lurks for them
both in and outside of their group, today's pious Jews must
exercise a twofold vigilance. They are like soldiers caught up in
a civil war—surrounded by enemies on all sides. Any effort to
mitigate this or that rigor leads promptly to licentiousness and
assimilation. Today's pious Jews must enforce ever-stricter and
more rigorous measures in order to retain their historical role
and to raise a generation that will follow in their ways.

Thus, if worldly Jews dress in short garments, pious Jews
must stick to their long gaberdines. Since the former shave their
beards and sidelocks, the latter must let them grow as long as
possible. Worldly Jews have founded a number of organizations
to protect Jewish interests, but pious Jews must keep far away
from their activities. If pious Jews must choose between entering a church or a Reform temple, Rabbi Moshe Sofer judged

that they should enter a church—it represents less danger to them than does the temple, where scrolls of the Torah are kept and where people allegedly pray to the Jewish God. A new kind of segregation has been established among the most pious Jews—a segregation from modern Jews and their institutions. All the efforts of these Jews are now bent to this end.

Nor is there unity among the pious themselves. They too are divided into factions both in Israel and in the land of the Diaspora. Those belonging to the Mizrachi are willing to work with the modern Jews and their organizations. Those of the Agudas Yisroel, on the other hand, stay at a greater distance from the nonbelieving Jews, but they recognize the state of Israel and have representatives in the Knesset and often in the ruling government. Those Jews stand ready to work alongside heretic Jews just as pious Jews have had to consort with non-Jews throughout history. The fact is that heretic Jews are very capable and have set up the various funds which have made the Jewish state possible. To ignore them entirely would often be impracticable. So even the members of the Agudas Yisroel have made numerous compromises. Many have donned short garments. Others have trimmed beards and sidelocks. When the Germans began to make reparation payments to victims of Nazi persecution, the members of the Agudas Yisroel at first grimaced and called it blood money as despicable as idolatry. Later they relented. Non-Jews may be *treyf*, but their money is *kosher*. They applied this same principle to the "Jewish goy."

But the extremists of Orthodoxy—the Szatmar Hasidim, who came from Hungary to the United States, and, in Israel, the Naturei Karta, watchers of the city of Jerusalem, who wear fur-edged hats and high stockings—still contend that every step nearer to the modern Jew, no matter how small, is a path to corruption. It is not out of malice that the Szatmar rabbi calls the members of the Agudas Yisroel heretics and men of evil. The ultra-Orthodox Jew adheres to the principle that once the movement toward the other side is launched, total homogeneity can only be a matter of time.

What is the number of these extremists? Not large. Throughout the whole world it comes to perhaps 100,000. These Jews have never recognized the Jewish state. In Israel, they do not cast votes, nor have representatives in the Knesset. They do not speak modern Hebrew, but stick to the Yiddish of their grandfathers and great-grandfathers. They have rejected modern Jewishness and isolated themselves just as their ancestors isolated themselves from Spinoza and Uriel Acosta. The ultra-Orthodox Jews have unofficially excommunicated the modern Jew, although they themselves constitute a small minority among world Jewry. To them, we are all branches broken off from the Jewish trunk. They are convinced that our future is the obliteration of our Jewishness. They, few as they are, will maintain the yoke of our religion. They, the extremists, will be there to receive the Messiah.

Are they right, or do they represent an ossified sector of the Jewish community, an anachronism that time will disperse? Only history will tell. One thing is clear—their way of life is based on a profound religious logic and a historic reason. The long beards and sidelocks, the old-fashioned garments, and the clinging to all the rigors and customs are directed toward one purpose only—complete segregation from non-Jews, and even more from Jews who are heading toward ultimate disappearance. This segregation is as old as Jewish exile itself, and has maintained Jews through the two thousand years of their existence in the Diaspora.

Yiddish, the Language of Exile

It is an accepted tenet of both our religious and secular literature that the exile was a calamity for the Jewish people. "And because of our sins we have been exiled from our land."[1] Three times a day Jews pray that their eyes may see God's return to Zion. Some of the extreme Zionists have expressed the opinion that the almost two-thousand-year period of the Diaspora was nothing more than an error and a void in our history. Others have even tried to belittle what Jews have created in exile: the Talmud, the Midrash, the Commentaries, the *Zohar*. Of course, the religious Jew would never concur. The exile might have been a punishment or a state of imprisonment, but within this

The original Yiddish handwritten manuscript from which this translation appears to have been made was found in Singer's archives with the title "Der goles yid un yidish" (The Diasporic Jew and Yiddish). Joseph Sherman, the late Yiddish scholar who helped organize Singer's papers at the Ransom Center, added a note to the manuscript, saying that it was "*NOT* listed" in the bibliography prepared by Roberta Saltzman and was "probably not published." But, in English, this essay appeared in *Judaica Book News*, Spring/Summer 1976, and was reprinted in an album titled *Next Year in Jerusalem: Portraits of the Jew in the Twentieth Century*, edited by Douglas Villiers (New York: Viking Press, 1976) and in the special issue of *Yiddish: Modern Jewish Studies* dedicated to Singer (volume 14, issues 2–3, 2006). The Yiddish version appeared for the first time in the winter 2021 issue of *Der Veker*, a contemporary Hasidic journal edited by Feivel Greenberg. There are two English-language drafts, an earlier draft with handwritten corrections, and a second that appears to incorporate additional edits. This version combines missing elements from the second, which appear as endnotes, to give the fullest possible version.

frame great spiritual works were produced. The ghettos teemed with saints, mystics, geniuses.[2]

I was brought up in an exceedingly Orthodox home. My father was the rabbi in the Polish *shtetl* of Leoncin, where I was born. Later he became the head of a yeshiva in Radzymin, and still later a rabbi in Warsaw on Krochmalna Street. In our house,[3] being a Jew and a man were synonymous. When my father wanted to say, "A man must eat," he would say, "A Jew must eat." It was not chauvinism as we understand it today. My father did not begrudge the nations their lands, their cities, their armies and navies. But since Esau and Ishmael had an opportunity to receive the Torah and repudiated it, they surrendered the best of everything to the Jews. In our house, the yearning for the Messiah and[4] the Holy Land was the very air we breathed. The Temple would rise[5] and the Holy Tongue would be spoken again. Atheism would disappear. The dead would be resurrected. Our risen forefathers would teach Torah to Jewish children and reveal secrets to them which could not be found in any kabbalistic book. The good Gentiles would share in paradise and learn the truth.

The pious Jew could not view the exile as a void—an error. The exile was a link in religious evolution. Even if the exile was its weakest link, it is known that a chain is as strong as its weakest link.[6] Actually, Jews in exile had to employ a great deal of their inventiveness to adjust the ideas of the Bible to those of their time. Subconsciously they thought of the period of the Bible as adults thinks of their childhood. Abraham with his two wives, Sarah and Hagar; Isaac, who favored Esau because of the delicacies Esau prepared for his palate; Jacob with two sisters as wives and two concubines; the tribes who sold their brother Joseph into slavery; Simon and Levi, who murdered the people of Shechem; Yehudah, who went to a harlot and in so doing copulated with his daughter-in-law;[7] King David and his passion for Bathsheba and Abigail; Solomon with his thousand wives, one of whom was the daughter of a Pharaoh—all these heroes of the Bible were oddly out of tune with concepts of holiness developed by Jews in exile. The Talmud and the Commentaries continually had to explain and defend the behavior of these biblical heroes, their primitivism, their lust for life, and their "gentile" traits.

As a pupil in the *heder*, the Hebrew school, raised in a house where the notion of righteousness signified the curbing of one's appetites and an immersion in Torah, prayer, Kabbalah, and Hasidism, I never could comprehend why the great figures of the Bible were so bodily oriented, so warlike, so paganly hot-blooded. I was still very young when I assailed my parents with questions about those biblical ancestors who were supposed to be super-saints but in reality seemed not much better than the peasants of our times. My parents constantly assured me that the stories of the Bible were nothing more than fables and that they should not be interpreted literally. Even the Christians of later epochs were embarrassed by the hedonism of the patriarchs, their greed for the flesh, their clannishness, and most of all by the fact that life after death and resurrection were never mentioned in the Old Testament. Christian theologians could never make peace with the idea that the Song of Songs was nothing more than a love poem.[8] In my later years it became clear to me that only in exile did Jews grow up spiritually. A people who never stopped fighting off their belligerent neighbors, who waged countless wars, could not keep all the commandments of the Torah, and certainly could not have taken upon themselves the many restrictions that the rabbis had added generation after generation. Moses's demand that the Jews create a kingdom of priests and a holy nation could not have become a reality in ancient Israel. The Bible testifies again and again that from a purely religious point of view, our history was a failure. Our prophets kept bemoaning this fact. Our kings, with a few exceptions, served idols and indulged in the abominations of their neighbors. The truth is that a people who must fight for its existence and be ever prepared for war cannot live by high religious ideals. The division between the aggressor and the attacked is seldom clear-cut. Christianity has often failed not because Christians are by nature hypocrites, but because they have never abandoned the ambitions of statehood. The kingdom of Heaven and the kingdom of Earth simply could not go together. The preacher of love and the bearer of the sword are the greatest contrasts the human mind can entertain. Even fighting for a just cause must turn into evil, since so often the innocent are punished for the misdeeds of the guilty.

Jewishness would never have reached its religious heights had the Jews remained in their land. Endless wars and ever-repeating occupations by stronger neighbors would eventually have transformed the Jews into an Arab tribe. This is a terrible statement to make but a true one nevertheless. If in the eight hundred years of independence ten tribes of Israel were lost, three thousand years of independence would have destroyed or crippled our spiritual heritage. Jews were able to reach the height of their religiosity only because for many centuries they were not drafted into any army and did not need to take part in the murderous battles of their captors—because they were almost completely isolated from the nations among whom they subsisted as despised strangers. Only because the Jews enjoyed a minimum of worldliness could they acquire a maximum of piety. The exiled Jews were aware of this, and they never aspired to be restored to their former state. Their Messianic hopes meant a pan-Jewishness, where all nations would recognize

God and submit to his reign. In all the religious disputes between Jews and Christians, the Jews' answer to their adversaries
was that if Jesus were the Messiah, he would have brought to an
end bloodshed among his followers. The fact that even popes
waged war and instigated battles among Christians was the
Jew's mightiest argument against all the Christian contentions
that Christianity had saved the world. Christians have never
found an answer to this.

I was born and brought up in a time when the Enlightenment
had its greatest victory among the Jews. In a sense, Poland was
the last fortress of what the Gentiles call the Talmudic Jew. The
Enlightenment came to the Jews in Germany and even Lithu-
ania scores of years before it reached Poland. Hasidism pre-
served the piety of the Polish Jews for the longest period. But
in my time Hasidism was already on the wane, and the ever-
encroaching Enlightenment succeeded in its two schools—the
one that preached total assimilation and the other that encouraged a new form of Jewish nationalism. Zionism was a product
of the latter.

Since at an early age I forsook the code of laws according to
which I was raised, and assimilation never appealed to me, I
automatically became a believer in Zionism. But I always realized that Zionism was and must remain a secular movement.
Regardless of how much a Jewish state would tolerate religious
Jews, it would not be the Jewish state they have prayed for in
the long night of exile. The proud Jews who defend their country, defy their enemies, seek friends among the nations, and try
to emulate their cultures, bring the Jews back to their biblical
beginnings, not to the End of Days. They are compelled to
make an end to their isolation, to their feelings of uniqueness,
their abhorrence of the pagan world and its pleasures—an isolation which sustained them for the last two thousand years of

their history. There is a contradiction between the Jewish state of exile and Jewish statehood that can never be ignored or glossed over. Even though I have never been an active Zionist, I have been bothered by this historical paradox.

Being brought up as an exiled Jew, I never felt that I was to blame for the actions of my gentile co-citizens. Until I was about twelve years old, I was a citizen of Russia. It never occurred to me that I was responsible for the Tsar's conquests in Central Asia or for the war with Japan. When Poland gained its independence, I never felt that I was guilty for the way the Polish government acted toward the Ukrainians, White Russians, and certainly not for its mistreatment of us Jews. I identify myself with the United States more than I ever did with the Russians or Poles, but even here I do not have the feeling that it is I who took California away from the Mexicans.

To the exiled Jew, politics was unkosher. I was happy as a boy when I read about Kerensky's revolution in Russia and the downfall of the Tsar, but it never dawned on me for a minute that it was my revolution. Later came the October Revolution, the pogroms in Ukraine, the Soviet persecution of all Jews who did not agree one hundred percent with their program, and all that I could feel was the eternal Jewish revulsion for violence.

The revolution in Russia and the Balfour Declaration came almost at the same time, and this was also the time that I decided my fate as a writer. In the city of Warsaw, where my father was a rabbi, Russian, then German, and then Polish had been the official languages since the time of my birth, but I did not speak one of them properly. My choice had to be between Yiddish and Hebrew, but neither of them was then a language in the accepted sense of the word. In 1918, Hebrew was still a language of prophets, of religious books, and of authors who preached nationalism, worldliness, and secularism in a biblical language and style. Hebrew had many festive and solemn idioms, but not enough everyday words, and no technological ones.⁹ After many trials I decided that I could not convey in Hebrew a conversation between a boy and a girl on Krochmalna Street, or even the talk used by the litigants who came to my father's courtroom. I turned to Yiddish, but I soon realized that this language had limitations and peculiarities inherent perhaps to no other language. Yiddish was never spoken by military men, police, people of power and influence. It was the language of the tailor, the storekeeper, the Talmud teacher, the rabbi, the matchmaker, the servant girl, but never of the engineer, the scientist, the army officer, the judge, the *grande dame*. No one could have written a *War and Peace*, an *Anna Karenina*, or even a *Crime and Punishment* in Yiddish because no counts, ranking officers, or even university students used Yiddish in their everyday life.

Yet Yiddish was the language of the Ashkenazic Jewish exile. It was remarkably appropriate not only to my experience but also to my spirit. Yiddish had a *Weltanschauung* of its own. It was saying: one cannot go through life straight and directly, one can only sneak by, muddle through, smuggle one's way. The leitmotif of Yiddish was that if a day passes without a misfortune, it is a miracle from Heaven. This is how Jews in Eastern Europe thought and felt whether they were rich, half poor, or paupers. Poverty lies in the very marrow of Yiddish. It is the language of those who are afraid, not those who arouse fear.

During the years when I was becoming a writer, both Hebrew and Yiddish made an effort to free themselves of their linguistic boundaries. In the last fifty years, Hebrew has become the official language of a state, a language used in universities, in laboratories, in an army and a navy, by bankers and diplomats, and even by Arabs in Israel. In half a century, Hebrew has become rejuvenated and worldly. Hebrew words no longer draw the same associations from the Bible, the Mishnah, the Midrash. It is no longer a holy tongue but a language as secular as English, Russian, or French.

The leftist Yiddishists tried to identify Yiddish with the social revolution. For a short time, a specially modernized Yiddish waved the red flag in Russia, in Poland, and in the United States. It preached materialism, bloody uprisings, revolutions, barricades. In their Marxist jargon, a rabbi became a cleric, a merchant a bourgeois, a wealthy person an exploiter, a peasant who made a living a kulak. Russia had promised its Jews a Yiddishist cultural autonomy and even an autonomous republic, Birobidzhan. The works of Marx, Lenin, Bukharin, and Stalin were translated into Yiddish. The Hebrew words used in Yiddish were written phonetically. A number of letters of our old Jewish alphabet were liquidated. In Yiddish, which was for hundreds of years the language of the *shtetl*, poems and essays were published that condemned the *shtetl* and its culture to oblivion.[10] But the powers that decide the fate of things decreed that this kind of Yiddish flourishing should not endure.[11] Stalin's antisemitism and the Soviet policy of supporting the enemies of the Jews all over the world finished, once and for all, the hopes of the Yiddish communists in Soviet Russia and everywhere else. It seems to be the destiny of Yiddish to remain what it always has been, a language of exile.

It could be said that Hebrew succeeded and Yiddish failed, but for me Yiddish is far from being a failure. By discarding its foreign trappings, its worldly chaff, and preserving the vitamins and hormones that nourished the language for generations, Yiddish is again slowly becoming what it was in its beginning—a language of Jewishness, the expression of those who still view human behavior from the point of view of kosher and nonkosher, permitted and forbidden.

For me and for many Jews, both in Israel and in the Diaspora, the exile and its various cultural media are still fulfilling their historical mission. Without two thousand years of total dedication to our heritage, neither Diaspora Jews nor Israelis would exist today.[12] As for Yiddish, it was and still is the language of study in a great many yeshivas all over the world. It is still spoken by the Hasidim in the Mea Shearim quarter of Jerusalem and by many other Ashkenazic Jews who adhere to the teachings of the Talmud and the *Shulchan Aruch*, to the wisdom of *muser*, and to the mysteries of the Kabbalah. To many Jews for whom Hebrew will remain forever a holy tongue, Yiddish may serve as the everyday language of *Yidishkayt*. As a matter of fact, Yiddish may become what Hebrew was for centuries—an esoteric religious language. At the time when the Talmud was written, Aramaic was considered a secular language. According to the Talmud, the angels don't understand Aramaic. But in the Middle Ages, when Hebrew was known to many and Aramaic to a few, the latter became the linguistic medium of the kabbalist and therefore also of the angels, seraphim, cherubim, and *arelim*. It is quite possible that the Moshe de León of the future may choose to write his *Zohar* in Yiddish.

Strange as this may sound, Yiddish literature has better chances to remain Jewish in content and form than modern Hebrew literature, which tries so hard to follow the literary vogues of the Gentiles and to take on all their idiosyncrasies. As a Jewish writer, I am shocked to see modern Hebrew literature becoming more and more worldly. The modern Jew's ambition to be "like all nations" at a time when the nations are becoming a hodgepodge of cultures, a generation like that which built the tower of

Babel, deprives modern Hebrew literature of the very juices that sustained its vitality.

Like my pious ancestors, I am waiting for a miracle, for a messiah and a redemption. Powers must arise that will instill a new purpose in our lives, a new faith, new reservoirs of individuality. An order must come in which peoples will cooperate economically and still uphold their individual unique traditions. A time must arrive when cultures will have no need of armies to defend their uniqueness and when the majorities will no longer attempt to swallow up the minorities. I cling to Yiddish because this language expresses my hope for redemption. When all nations realize that they are in exile—exile will cease to be. When majorities discover that they too are minorities, the minority will be the rule and not the exception. Yiddish-speaking Jews—with their fear of physical and spiritual effacement, their desperate effort to sustain the values and the languages of their history, their struggle for independence and their actual dependence on the good will of others—these Jews symbolize to me the whole human species. People must be both themselves and integrated parts of a whole, loyal to their own homes and origins and deeply cognizant of the origins of others. They must possess both the wisdom of doubt and the fire of faith. In a world where we are all basically strangers, the commandment "And thou shalt love thy stranger" is not just an altruistic wish, but the very core of our existence.

Jewish art in general, and Yiddish art in particular, must express these truths. To the Yiddish artist, yesterday is as actual as today. Those who died are not dead. Destroyed cities still teem with life. For me and those like myself, two thousand years of exile have been not a dark passage into nowhere, but a grand experiment in sustaining a people only on spiritual values. Even though we have attained the land we longed for and revived the Hebrew language, the experiment of exile is far from being concluded.[13]

The Hitlers, the Mussolinis, and the Stalins turn to dust, but the works of the spirit are ever imbued with new life.[14] Such mighty powers as the Assyrian and Babylonian empires left nothing to posterity but their names and some crumbling artifacts, but the children of Israel have been creative for thousands of years and have even performed the miracle of national rebirth.[15] To me, the Jews and their history lead the way for the future.[16]

I am not exaggerating when I say that, of all Jews, those who spoke Yiddish were and still are the least known. But the very fact that for generations Yiddish was despised should serve as a sign that great treasures of folklore, wisdom, and uniqueness are hidden in it. Yiddish shared and is still sharing the lot of those Jews who resigned from the promises of this world, with its vanities and its wickedness. They will remain hidden until there will be justice for all. A lot of what is to be learned about such Jews can be found in Yiddish literature.

Yiddish Theater Lives,
Despite the Past

I was already a young writer and an ardent reader of world literature when I began to attend plays in Yiddish. Some of them were written by Polish- or Russian-Jewish playwrights, and many of them were imported from the golden land of America. I could see even then that we had not produced in Yiddish a Shakespeare, a Molière, or a Strindberg. These plays were folkish, utterly naive and sometimes even ridiculous, but I enjoyed them and often laughed, not as much at the banal subject matter, but at the clumsiness of the writers, directors, and even the actors.

I learned later in life that many non-Yiddish plays had the same faults. They were constructed from the same flimsy stuff as the Yiddish ones. It was true that every Yiddish play needed a heart-rending recital of Kaddish and a wedding ceremony in order to keep the noisy audiences quiet for some time. But I was

This essay first appeared in English in *The New York Times* on January 20, 1985 (section 2, page 1). Two drafts exist in the archives, one corrected yet incomplete, and a second incorporating Singer's edits and including a few additional corrections. In both cases, the draft begins with the question, "Are we experiencing a revival of Yiddish theater today?" The first five paragraphs appear to have been added later, perhaps in answer to a request by the piece's commissioning editor. No Yiddish original has been found.

told that in almost every second or third English play there was a body of someone just murdered, with Scotland Yard trying to find the culprit. It seemed that the theater thrived on clichés and wishful thinking everywhere.

If someone were to ask me what was essentially the topic of Yiddish theater, I would say it was basically a love story—the tale of human love oppressed by religious asceticism and supposedly freed in an epoch of enlightenment. The protagonists of both the Yiddish theater and Yiddish literature were young men and women of the *shtetl* who refused to marry by arranged marriages and wanted to follow their own romantic desires. They craved to free themselves from their poverty-stricken and backward environment. They yearned for the big world, for secular education, and for the right to wear modern clothes, to do away with the caftan, the wig, and the whole burden of Orthodoxy, which they considered Asiatic.

The villains of the Yiddish plays, as a rule, were Russian oppressors and Jewish religious fanatics. The most humorous character in these plays was of course the matchmaker. He was invariably dressed in shabby clothes, snuffed tobacco, sneezed and spat a lot of nonsense. To make him even funnier, he was often a stammerer and sometimes hard of hearing. He almost always tried to marry off a young girl of seventeen with a tottering old man who could have been her great-grandfather, but she was in love with an emancipated young man, and love finally triumphed.

A Yiddish play, like any other play, had to have a happy ending. In the Polish and Russian kitsch plays, the young lover might have been a count or some other dignitary. He took the girl to his palace and there they lived happily ever after. There was little hope in the Jewish ghettos for young couples, and a happy ending was immigration to America. In many of the Yiddish plays which I have seen, the groom or bride discover that they have a rich uncle in New York who turns up at the wedding dressed in a top hat and a tuxedo with a check for $20,000. The thrill of this event is overwhelming, especially if the bride is a poor orphan. Usually, there is a would-be seducer who wants the girl for himself, although he has a wife and a house full of children.

Are we experiencing a revival of Yiddish theater today? If we are, what could be the reason for it? Did the Yiddish theater possess artistic values that merit a place in the theater lore of our time?

One cannot speak about the Jewish theater without taking into consideration that for thousands of years the theater was for the Jews an institution of idolatry and corruption. These notions still linger among the extremely pious. I remember my father saying in one of his sermons, "The wicked sit day and night in a theater, eat pork, and sin with loose women." It is worth noting that when the great Spinoza wanted to describe in his *Ethics* unrestrained merriment and worldly pleasures, he specified the theater and the use of perfume. Spinoza was given a traditional Jewish education, and the theater and perfume represented to him indulgence in pleasures. Since the Jews were forbidden "to make unto thee a graven image or any likeness of anything that is in Heaven above," the art of imitating people might also have been looked upon as a form of idolatry. Besides, according to Mosaic law, a man was not allowed to dress in woman's garment and vice versa. This too could have hindered the development of any theater among the Jews. King Herod broke all traditions and built an amphitheater in the city of Jerusalem where Greek dramas were performed. After the destruction of the Second Temple and the dispersion of the Jews, there were neither the conditions nor the mood for theater. Jews had to constantly fight for their physical and spiritual survival.

There were some exceptions. The Talmud mentions a Purim festival in Babylonia including elements of pantomime. They used to burn a figure of Haman that was strapped to a wooden hoop. After much frolicking and dancing, the remnants of the figure were thrown into the river. In the year 408, the Eastern Roman Emperor Theodosius II forbade this Purim spectacle. Similar festivities were practiced in Yemen and in Caucasia, to which Jews migrated even before the Roman invasion. And after the Jewish exile from Spain and the migration to German and Gallic lands, the Jews put on extensive Purim *shpils* (plays) in German cities, and Hannukah *shpils* as well. The story of the tyrant Ahasuerus, the evil Haman, the Jewish statesman Mordecai, and his beautiful cousin Esther who saved the Jews from a holocaust, was too rich and dramatic a story to be overlooked as material for playacting. Purim was the only holiday where getting drunk was considered a *mitzvah*.

Even in my time, when I was a child in Warsaw, masked boys used to come to our house on Purim to play the characters in the book of Esther. Sometimes they sang songs of which my father did not approve. He was always in a rush to give these performers their few groschen and let them go. For us children all this was sheer delight.

The first Yiddish plays of any artistic value were written in Yiddish or German-Yiddish between 1790 and 1830 and were a product of the *Haskalah*, the Jewish Enlightenment, such as *Reb Henoch* by Isaac Euchel (1756–1814), *Frivolousness and Bigotry* by Aaron Wolfasohn (1754–1835), *The Deceitful World* by I. B. Levinsohn (1788–1860), *The First Jewish Recruit* by Israel Aksenfeld (1797–1866), and in later years, *Serkele* by Solomon Ettinger (1802–1856) and *The Scarf* by Abraham Ber Gottlober (1811–1899). Most of these plays were not performed or published until many years later and went from hand to hand in manu-script form.

Abraham Goldfaden (1840–1908) is considered the father of Jewish theater. He wrote some forty plays, directed them, and acted in them as well. One of them, *The Two Kuni Lemels,* is being performed right now in New York while these lines are being written. Goldfaden attracted to his company a number of would-be actors who played and sang in wine cellars and tav-erns in Romania and Galicia and wherever they could find an audience. They called themselves the Broder Singers—after the town of Brody, where some of them originated. A handful of them were folk musicians, *klezmerim,* and klezmer music too is going through a sort of revival in the United States, in Israel, and in some European cities. Abraham Goldfaden and his part-ner Israel Godner, also an actor, discovered a prolific play-wright, Joseph Lateiner. He produced some eighty plays and in the late years of the nineteenth century became a leader and promoter of Jewish theater in America.

After the assassination of Tsar Alexander II in 1881, and the pogroms that followed, Jews from Russia and Poland began to immigrate to America in masses, Abraham Goldfaden among them. As a result, the Yiddish theater flourished for many years in the New World. The demand for plays seemed to inspire new talent. In time, many of these productions were brought back to Europe. One of these immigrant playwrights, Jacob Gordin, specialized in adapting the works of classic European writers for the Yiddish stage. He adapted the works of Lessing, Schiller, Goethe, and Shakespeare's *King Lear,* which he called *The Jew-ish King Lear.* One of Gordin's original plays, *Mirele Efros,* was performed in Warsaw by Esther Rachel Kaminska and later by her daughter Ida Kaminska.

For millions of Jewish immigrants, mostly hardworking people, many of them half illiterate, the Yiddish theater was a well of entertainment and a source of information about the great world, the United States of America, Jewish history, and many things of which they had never heard in the old country. As Abe Cahan, the late editor of the *Jewish Daily Forward* used to say, "The Yiddish press and the Yiddish theater must teach these immigrants how to use a handkerchief."

Abe Cahan, himself an immigrant from Vilna, had become an American novelist and the most important critic of the Yiddish theater. He demanded that both the Yiddish press and the theater be strictly realistic and totally comprehensible by the theatergoers and readers. His criterion was whether the elevator man of the Forward building could understand and enjoy the article or the play in question. When Cahan wrote in a review that a play was too complex to be appreciated by the elevator man, it was taken off stage. Of course, the elevator man was happy to comply, and his answer was always, "No, Mr. Cahan, I cannot understand it. The whole thing is over my head."

Nevertheless, Yiddish theater brought out and encouraged quite a number of talents over the years, writers such as Peretz Hirschbein, David Pinski, Leon Kobrin, Zalmon Libin, and Fischel Bimko, and such actors as Rudolph Schildkraut and his son Joseph, Jacob Adler, Keni Liptzin, Ludwig Satz, Sigmund Mogulesco, Jacob Ben-Ami, Berta Gersten, Muni Wiesenfeld (who later became Paul Muni), David Kessler, Julius Adler, and such stars as Boris Thomashefsky, Maurice Schwartz, Menashe Skulnik, Molly Picon, Clara Young, Bessie Thomashefsky, and Celia, Luther, and Stella Adler—all children of the great Jacob Adler—and many, many others. Yiddish theater in the late 1880s and '90s, and in the early 1920s and '30s, had become a binding passion for millions of Jewish immigrants. Boris

Thomashefsky became an object of hero worship for many Yiddish-speaking women. It was said that one woman threw herself before his carriage to express her infinite admiration and love.

For many years, Yiddish theater kept growing in the United States, in Poland, in Russia, in Argentina. Goldfaden returned to Europe, and although he was the founder of the Yiddish theater, he himself lost his hold on it and was utterly neglected everywhere. He died a forgotten man in 1908. For a long time the Yiddish theater in Poland, in Russia, and everywhere else depended on the plays and "stars" from America. During World War I, Yiddish theater was forbidden in Russia. After the Bolshevik Revolution, the Yiddish theater came back to life under the leadership of Aleksandr Granovsky. The Soviets were eager to show their interest in developing the cultures of minorities and provided Granovsky with a modern studio and a theater where the walls were painted by the already famous Marc Chagall. The communists refused to depend on American plays and their stars. The Soviet Yiddish theater had brought out a star of their own, Solomon Mikhoels. They performed works by Sholem Aleichem, Mendele Moykher Sforim, Peretz, and by the Yiddish poet Peretz Markish, who in later years was given the Stalin Prize and still later, in the time of the Stalin purges, was liquidated together with the same Mikhoels and a number of other Yiddish writers.

Through the years some good things happened to the Yiddish theater. In 1907, Sholem Asch's *God of Vengeance* was translated into German and performed by the famous Max Reinhardt. Maurice Schwartz founded the Yiddish Art Theater and had many successes. The greatest of them was perhaps *Yoshe Kalb*, by my late brother I. J. Singer. New playwrights had emerged like H. Leivick, Osip Dymov, Alter Kacyzne, Aaron Zeitlin, Jacob Prager, and Harry Sackler. One of the biggest successes in Yiddish theater was Ansky's *Dybbuk*, which played in the 1920s all over Europe. There were some optimists who believed Yiddish theater still had a long life ahead. However, millions of Jewish children grew up in America, both North and South, as well as in Russia, Poland, Romania, and all over Europe, without any knowledge of Jewish history, Yiddish, or Hebrew. Some Yiddishists considered Yiddish a language with a mission to help the masses in bringing about socialism or communism, and then disappear. Abe Cahan was one of them. Yiddish was snubbed by the assimilationists and also by the Zionists, for whom Hebrew was the real Jewish language and Yiddish only some corrupted German dialect. The Wall Street crash and the depression that followed convinced many young Jews in the United States that communism was the only solution to the Jewish problem. It was a consensus that Yiddish was dying slowly but surely.

When I came to the United States in 1935, Yiddish was already on its way out. An additional tragedy of the Yiddish theater was the fact that Yiddish writers as a rule did not write plays. Most of the dramas were adaptations from novels or stories. The theater had to rely on kitsch. I remember my brother saying to me once, "If you ever intend to write a play, do it now, because in a year or two it might be too late." Hitler was already in power in Germany, and a Second World War was imminent. How strange that in Warsaw and in Lodz they played Yiddish theater almost to the very day of the Hitler invasion. As a matter of fact, they played Yiddish theater in the Hitler ghettos between one death-action and another.

For a man who began his career as a writer in such circumstances, it is not easy to be optimistic. Although Yiddish theater still exists here in America and in Israel, and even though I myself am foolish enough to dabble in it, I wouldn't dare say that we were witnessing a revival or that one may occur in the near future. But the very fact that Yiddish literature and the Yiddish theater are not completely forgotten proves that resignation is not an attribute of Jewishness. We still have some writers and I still see from time to time such Yiddish actors and actresses as Joseph Buloff, the great comedian Leo Fuchs, Seymour Rexite, Miriam Kressyn, Dina Halpern, Pesach Burstein and his wife Lillian Lux and son Mike Burstyn, Zvee Scooler, and some others who just refuse to give up Yiddish.

It is hard to believe that there exist a number of young people who even take Yiddish seriously and who try to build an artistic career on it. These young people know by instinct that the Jews have never given up their spiritual values. We carried away our books from the Inquisition and the auto-da-fé. We are still teaching Jewishness in some hideouts in Soviet Russia, Syria, Ethiopia, Iran, Iraq, and similar such places. Even Hitler did not succeed in destroying our literature, both religious and secular.

I don't really look forward with nostalgia for a renewal of the Yiddish theater I knew because I am convinced that the Yiddish theater has never really died. It has entered like a dybbuk into many Broadway plays and musicals and into a great number of Hollywood movies and television productions as well. What I would really like is not a revival of the old theater, but a changed approach to the very essence of theater, which should be treated as an integral part of the great art of storytelling.[1]

Of one thing I am sure, that if we are ever blessed with a renewal of our theater, it will not be a product of enlightenment, atheism, self-hatred, and self-mockery. It will be rather a product of faith in God and Jewish immortality as were the Purim and Hanukkah *shpils* in Babylonia, in Germany, in Holland, and wherever Jews managed to remain themselves despite all persecutions. We will not need to import Greek idolatrous dramas as did King Herod. There is great drama in the struggle between good and evil, justice and exploitation, the power of reason and the emotions so well described in our books of *muser*, or morality.[2] Free choice is still the greatest gift God has bestowed upon humanity, and the effort it takes to make use of this inexhaustible treasure is connected with more drama and suspense than any theater of atheism and cynicism could ever devise.

Yiddish and Jewishness

Like grammar, nature has no exceptions. If something in nature appears to us as an exception, it means that the general law is yet unknown.

The Jewish people appears to be an exception among peoples. As Balaam said about the Israelites, "The people shall dwell alone and shall not be reckoned among the nations." In all the long history of our people, we have had our own country for only a relatively short time. We used to and continue to live in many different lands, just as we have spoken and still speak

The original typescript of this essay has only the handwritten word "Yiddisch" written across the top, as well as several illegible words crossed out. The Yiddish original has not been found. The English draft appears together with an article titled "Yidish un Yidishe literatur" (Yiddish and Yiddish Literature) and the date 1962, and Singer did indeed publish an article by this name in the special sixty-fifth anniversary issue of the *Forverts* (Dec. 30, section 5, page 17), but this article bears no textual relationship to this essay. There is also an article appearing in the *Forverts* titled "Yidish un Yidishkayt" (Yiddish and Yiddishkayt, March 13, 1960), for which an entry exists in the archive, but this is not the same as the untitled English essay either. The title adopted above takes into account the different historical concerns involved as well as the topic of the essay itself. There are several drafts in the archive, including a corrected typescript and a clean typescript which appears to be a draft or two later. The version included here reflects the latest available draft while incorporating some crossed-out sections when relevant. Perhaps most notably, the main difference between the versions consists in how Singer refers to the Jewish people—in the third-person plural in the earlier draft, and in first-person plural in the later draft. The move from "they" to "we" considerably changes the tone—though the content remains largely the same.

innumerable languages. Thousands of mighty states have perished since our history began. Many languages and cultures
have been forgotten. But we continue to live and show the
power of resurrection. Only now, after two thousand years, have
we begun to build up our ancient land. We have revived the
Hebrew language, which for two thousand years was considered dead. We brought Aramaic with us into the Diaspora, a
language which is spoken by no one today, and which has sur-
vived at all because of us. Our Hebrew scholars up to the present day have written in a mixture of Hebrew and Aramaic.
Both the Talmud and the *Zohar* are written in Aramaic, and so
are our marriage contracts and divorce papers.

The world has exact ideas of what constitutes a nation, but
the existence of the Jewish people has made a mockery of these
ideas. Jews are Jews whether they live in Tel Aviv or in New
York. They are the same if they speak Hebrew, Yiddish, Arabic,
or Ladino. The endless ruminations on the issue of Jewishness
as a religion, race, or nationality have come to no definite con-
clusions. Jews may have blond hair, speak Russian, be French
citizens, or consider themselves atheist, but they are still Jews.

Where the facts do not fit a theory, the theory has to be
changed. But there are maniacs who, when the facts fail to conform to a theory, get angry with the facts. As an anecdote goes
about a German professor: when he was told that the facts do
not confirm his theory, he cried out, "It's the fault of the facts!"
This is the way many of our enemies have thought, from Haman
up to the present day, in their theories about us. Jews have given
the greatest disappointment to Soviet theorists, since Jews and
their existence do not conform to the theories of Leninism.

Among the hundreds of people who enunciate theories of
Judaism, I too have my theory, which is the product of my own
personal reflection upon the Jewish people. My theory is that

Jewishness is not a constant value or phenomenon, but something similar to a mathematical function whose minimum is infinitely small and maximum is infinitely large. There are small Jews and large Jews, and some Jews who try to approach zero but somehow can never reach it.[1] Also, I think that Jewishness has a number of dimensions—don't ask me how many. There is in mathematics a concept which is called the continuum, whose symbol is the letter *alef*. The Jew is a continuum but of such a kind that all the letters of the alphabet are not sufficient to express it.

What is true about the Jew in this regard is true, in my opinion, of all nations, of all humanity. But I will speak about this later.

We have had in our history many different periods through which our value as Jews kept changing, but as a rule we have aspired toward the maximum rather than the minimum. If we regressed for a period in our history, there was then a reaction and we moved forward. If we neglected one side of Jewishness at one time, we then developed another. In order not to lose our individuality as a people, we needed, among other things, a language of our own. But at certain times in our history, one language did not suffice. We needed more than one language to express our essence as a people. The phenomenon of multilingualism is not so rare in history. Educated people in the Middle Ages knew not only their own languages, but Latin and often ancient Greek. Later, the European aristocracy knew their own languages, the classical languages, and also French. History has demanded that Jews, to develop themselves to the maximum, speak Hebrew, Yiddish, Aramaic, and sometimes other languages too. The idea that Hebrew excludes Yiddish, or that Yiddish is hostile to Hebrew, is completely false. To ignore Yiddish means ignorance of six hundred years of Jewish history. It means ignorance of our commentaries, the kabbalists of Eastern

Europe, the creators of Hasidism, the Enlightenment, Zionism, Yiddish literature, and many other achievements of our culture and religion. The Yiddish idiom has penetrated so deeply into Hebrew that one cannot understand modern Hebrew if one doesn't know Yiddish.

It is characteristic of both Yiddish and Hebrew to serve both religious and secular purposes. The two kinds of Jews—those who aspired to the minimum and those who aspired to the maximum—have employed both Hebrew and Yiddish. The Talmudic law that forbids the reading of secular books proves that even in ancient times there was a secular literature in Hebrew. Our sages doubted whether the book of Ecclesiastes should be included among the holy books, considering it belonging to the category of secular literature. The inclination to worldliness and assimilation is as old as the Jewish people. It began in Egypt, and accompanied the Israelites into the desert, and it was this inclination which produced the Golden Calf. It is clear that the assimilationists have always had their literature, their preachers, and their prophets.

The same has been true of Yiddish. Its worldly literature is as old as its religious literature. The so-called "*shpilman* period," the epoch of the bard, and the "*muser* period," the epoch of morality, were contemporaneous. Nor is it an accident that the creators of worldly literature in Hebrew were also the creators of the worldly Yiddish literature. Yiddish and Hebrew together were the languages of Ashkenazi Jews for the last six hundred years. From the beginning, there were differences between the Yiddish and Hebrew secular literatures, but the similarities were very great. The creators of both literatures were possessed by the same ideas—that the Jews should become like all the other nations of the world. Both literatures criticized religious dogmas and customs, Jewish dress, the Jewish way of making a living, and so on.

Both literatures tried to open a window to the world for the Jews, preached a broader, more worldly education, and pointed to Western Europe and its culture as an example.

Under their influence, millions of Jews stopped wearing their long gaberdines, shaved off their beards, and began to send their children to secular schools. The readers of these secular literatures reared a generation of assimilationists. Strange and paradoxical as it sounds, most of the readers of modern Hebrew and Yiddish literature raised children that knew neither language. This process still continues today. In the United States, Soviet Russia, and all over the world, millions of Jews vehemently aspire in the direction of minimum Jewishness. How strange that both literatures that were created out of Jewish uniqueness, that express so much of our individuality, should lead to the opposite pole—namely, to imitate non-Jews, to use their languages, to penetrate their culture, and to forget Jewish culture and heritage. No matter how rich in individuality a literature is and how deeply it is rooted in a national soil, if its tendency is toward assimilation, it will use and diffuse its national energy for that purpose.[2] A locomotive needs as much energy to go backwards as to go forwards. More effort is required to commit suicide than to go on living.

I would not be here speaking about Jewish literature if the Jewish tendency to advance and to renew itself had not shown its might in the last years. The desire to be like everyone else not only has meant assimilation and estrangement, but it has also brought with it the yearning for a national home. Since all other nations have their own land, the Jews must have their land too. Here the paradox has revealed itself: a will to be similar to others has brought with it a national reawakening. It has already been pointed out that from the beginning, the Enlightenment moved in two directions: toward absolute assimilation and toward Jewish nationalism.[3] The motive idea behind the latter movement was that, since complete assimilation is impossible, we must have our own territory to lead a full worldly life. Exile and worldliness do not go well together. I once heard a speaker in a small town say, "In exile, we can't even live the life of a Gentile. If we want to live like the Gentiles, we have to have a country of our own." There was an uncanny truth in these words.

Yiddish literature has contributed to Zionism no less than Hebrew. Both literatures combined to make the Zionist dream a reality, by exhibiting all the shortcomings and misfortunes inherent of exile. When the Jews were finally rewarded with their homeland, Yiddish literature was excluded and Hebrew became the literature of the renewed normalized nation. Hebrew found its home and address in Israel, and Yiddish consequently became weaker and more homeless. One could compare the fate of Yiddish to the part of the army that is assigned to fight in the front ranks so that the larger part of the army can build up a fortified position. Yiddish literature was left to carry on the battle against assimilation. This happened at a time following the annihilation of almost all of Eastern European Jewry.

Never has Yiddish suffered so much from being in exile as in the present. The younger generation neither speaks nor studies Yiddish, and the older generation is disillusioned and often indifferent to it. One sometimes has the feeling that Yiddish literature and language have done their jobs and fate has condemned them to death—like the drones that fly from the hive to fertilize the queen but are not allowed to return to the hive. Some feel that the last hope for the survival of Yiddish literature is that it be translated into Hebrew. It is often prophesied that Yiddish must suffer the same fate of annihilation as the Jews of Eastern Europe.

Such a fate would be especially cruel, for Yiddish literature still remains richer in creative power than Hebrew. It may well be that the number of readers is diminishing, but this is not the case with the creative well which continues to irrigate the Jewish garden, and which is still full of enriching powers. Strange as it may sound, the Yiddish language becomes more alive all the time. Such writers as J. J. Trunk, I. J. Singer, A. M. Fuchs, and many others, have stirred up the hidden linguistic treasures of Yiddish. Some other writers have revived old Yiddish. As for the poets, Aaron Zeitlin, Abraham Sutzkever, and Itzik Manger have added to the Yiddish language, each in his own fashion. Before the outbreak of the Second World War, there were such writers in Poland as Joseph Perle, I. Zhitnitsky, and Efraim Kaganovsky. Not a day passes without new Yiddish words and unknown idioms being discovered. Yiddish, like English, is still spoken in over half of the world. Yiddish is very rich in synonyms and especially words and expressions signifying character. I myself have written down hundreds of words and phrases on the margins of Stuchkov's *Thesaurus of Yiddish*. I doubt if the great Yiddish dictionary which is now being composed will exhaust the Yiddish language in all of its ten volumes. Is there no other future for Yiddish than oblivion?

I have meditated a great deal on these problems and I came to a conclusion that I will try here to briefly define.

At first glance, Yiddish does indeed look doomed. The Polish Jews and the other masses who spoke Yiddish no longer exist, and most American Jews bring up their children to speak only English. I know that even the children who study Yiddish in the United States and Argentina will not grow up to be natural readers of Yiddish. There is always more literature available in Spanish or in English than in Yiddish. These are the living languages, the languages of work, technique, business, careers. From a rational point of view, Yiddish is indeed lost, and must soon become part of the past. But does everything only happen rationally and realistically? Those who are acquainted with the history of the Jews know that our history has always been irrational. We have always been the exception that challenged the rule.

Jewish national and religious vitality has shown itself to be stronger than all external powers. Jewishness exists and will continue to exist. We know from our experience that Jewishness has had and will maintain its power of expression. Jews have borrowed words from other nations, but never a complete language. Even if Jews in Israel today had adjusted the facts to the theory and had become like all other nations, Jews in exile would remain mavericks, nonconformists, a kind of sociological antinomy, which indicates that the sociology of our time is no more than a temporary construction.

As far as I can see, the whole world aspires toward culture that will be less and less dependent on territory and more and more of an expression of the human need for individuality. If humanity were ever to become really free, the number of languages would have to become larger and not smaller. Not only would modern languages develop in this direction, but there would also be a resurrection of ancient languages. Even in our own time, languages have come to life—Hebrew, Lithuanian, Ukrainian, Belorussian, Gaelic, and many others. In Africa, many languages are now springing into existence that no one has ever heard of. Although we do not realize it, we live in a time of a cultural revival of great magnitude. I myself do not believe that Yiddish will die in the midst of this huge revival. Yiddish was, is, and can remain the language of Jewishness. Its existence does not depend on the number of schools and universities, but on the need for individuality, which can never die. The fate of

the Yiddish language depends totally on the Jewish creative
spirit, on those who cannot, and will not, make peace with assimilation. A single Thomas Edison brought light to the houses
of all nations. A score of prophets brought Jewishness to all
corners of the world. Jews must again work this kind of miracle.
They have again to make the impossible possible. There is a
saying, if you cannot go down, you must go up. Yiddish can
never become just another language like any other language, for
it has the potential to express the eternal Jewish spirit. Jews, like
all nations, live in a perpetual crisis. They are doomed—and a
doomed language is perhaps the proper way to express them.
From a rational point of view, even Jews in Israel are far from
being safe. In the time of the atomic bomb, when the caprice of
a maniac is enough to ignite the world, all people and all nations
are in exile.

In our time, the exception is becoming more and more the rule.
I would say that all nations are becoming more and more spiritually identified with the fate of the Jews. Their cultures are becoming as vulnerable and precarious as Yiddish. The problem facing
Yiddish culture is therefore mainly a problem of quality. The question is not whether we will have enough readers, but to what extent Yiddish can reflect Jews—their restless and disturbed spirit,
their eternal dissatisfaction, their disdain of the world and their
hunger for the world, their yearning for a home and their wander-
lust, their feeling for social justice and their inclination to acquire
privileges, their asceticism and their sensualism.

Even though Yiddish literature has advanced a great deal
during its short existence, it still remains almost provincial.
Mendele Moykher Sforim, Sholem Aleichem, Abraham Reisen,
Dovid Bergelson, A. M. Fuchs, and almost all other Yiddish
writers wrote about the *shtetl* and for the *shtetl*, even though
most Jews actually live in big cities. For some strange reason,

Yiddish literature has avoided the themes of the big city. There is little in Yiddish literature about Petersburg, Kiev, and even such Jewish cities as Warsaw, Vilna, Riga, and Odessa. In the United States, Jews in great masses have lived in Chicago, Detroit, New York, Philadelphia, but Yiddish literature in America has ignored those centers. There does not exist any real description of Jewish life in Paris, London, Rio de Janeiro, Johannesburg, or Buenos Aires, even though Jews live there in great numbers. Because Jewish literature originated in the *shtetl* and continued to express it origin, it has never reflected the Jewish political movements. Neither the Zionists nor the assimilationists, not even the Jewish socialists—those cosmopolitans and bleeders for all causes—could find themselves in Yiddish literature. And where does one find in Yiddish literature those Jews who made millions of dollars, who built the great department stores in all the great cities of the world? Where are the Rothschilds, the Einsteins, the Weizmanns, the Bergsons, the great number of converts? Even Hasidism did not find its image in our literature in full measure. We do not have novels about such personalities as Rabbi Israel of Rizhin, Rabbi Menahem from Vitebsk, the famous Rabbi Elimelech, and many other great and of colorful figures. And how about the underworld? Can we and should we deny the existence of our swindlers and thieves, the ill-famed procurers of Buenos Aires, Rio de Janeiro, and Istanbul? And on whose shoulders did such a man as Sergei Rubinstein grow up? Jewish life is one great unbelievable adventure which is unrolled in all corners of the globe, especially in the large cities, but our literatures, both Yiddish and Hebrew, have voluntarily put themselves into a ghetto. When one reads Yiddish and Hebrew literature, one gets the impression that all Jews live in small towns and all are small peddlers, coughing teachers, and women who deal in rotten apples. Sometimes one gets the feeling that our literatures have had the intention of awaking pity for the Jews, and of meeting accusations about Jews having an adventuring and acquisitive spirit. One must admit that in describing poverty, both physical and spiritual, our literature has been outstanding. But poverty is not a Jewish attribute, and many of these Jews from the *shtetls* have built and are still building skyscrapers in New York City, their children members of the English Parliament and the American Congress, and sometimes of the Politburo in Moscow. One never finds these Jews represented in our literature.

Some maintain that the Yiddish language itself is not sufficient to describe the Jewish adventure. They say that Yiddish was born in the ghetto and must die in the ghetto. But first of all, there is some proof to the contrary, and second, a language can expand and go beyond its original limits. Jews have actually done what Nietzsche demanded—transcended themselves. The whole of Jewish history is in a sense an illustration of Nietzsche's *Zarathustra*.

In his cycle of novels, Balzac sought to recreate the human comedy.[4] The very attempt at such an effort elevated French literature. Zola had the same tremendous ambition.[5] But no one has as yet undertaken the delineation of the Jewish comedy, or, if you prefer, the Jewish tragicomedy. True, to write such a work would require extraordinary knowledge and vast insight. And Jews seldom remain in the country of their birth. A character who is one day in Warsaw, the next in Paris, the week after in New York, and whose language and customs change with fantastic rapidity, presents a problem of the utmost difficulty to writers. Also, the drama of the Jew is often so melodramatic that writers fear telling the story. But no literature can afford to ignore its natural heroes. If Jewish life was and remains exciting, we must produce artists capable of dealing with these adventures. In a sense, all literatures today suffer from a similar malady. Most professional writers are of insufficient stature to comprehend their experience. They lack the awareness to deal either factually or spiritually with the life of the present generation. Even American literature suffers from a kind of provincialism. Neither Hemingway, Steinbeck, Faulkner, nor Tennessee Williams has encompassed in his art the tremendous adventure that is America. Jewish writers find themselves in the ghetto too—a ghetto of alcohol, obscenity, cheap sex, and vulgar sentimentality.

Instead of mourning our fate and brooding about who reads our books, we should concentrate all our energies upon the spiritual value of our writing. First let there be a book, and then we can search for a reader. Yiddish must orient itself in two directions, both of which it has avoided until now. First, it must become what it was intended to be, an instrument of Jewishness. Second, it must, in the name of Jewishness, encounter the world and all its vanities, illusions, temptations, and adventures. The prophet who wanted to save Nineveh could not remain in the bowels of the whale. He had to come to Nineveh and face it and its inhabitants. A literature that aspires nowadays to awaken and bind together the Jews of the world should not remain restricted to little towns and should not cultivate a primitivist attitude. Jews are not static but dynamic in their nature. If a revitalized Jewishness is destined to come into existence with meaning for modern Jews, it must be in the form of a great spiritual vision and awakening.

We do not have to be anxious about our voice being heard. Our worry should be whether our voice deserves to be heard. Do we really have something to say and to reveal? We do not have to doubt that there will be ears. The question is rather whether there will be music.

"The stone the builders rejected has now become the corner-stone" (Psalms 118:22). These words were spoken out of a deep human experience. Don't consider me a dreamer when I say that Yiddish literature, the literature of the Jews, has the potential to bring all literatures out of their present crisis. Our suffering is the suffering of the world, and the only difference is that for many reasons we feel it more deeply. Our adventure is the world's adventure. Humanity is now preparing to reach the Moon, Mars, and Venus. There is a possibility that we might meet there other rational creatures, that we may encounter objects for which we have neither a concept or a name. The human dictionary may have to be enlarged to hold God knows how many more nouns, adjectives, and verbs. A world language may have to be created, and the languages of the different nations may serve more and more for purely cultural purposes rather than as means for communications. All the separate, national languages may become things of the past. In other words, what Yiddish is today, an instrument of cultural individuality and attachment to tradition, other languages may become tomorrow.

We live in an epoch today of rapid changes, and we must be prepared for them. The discovery of the planets, the population explosion, birth control, and genetics are all changing the face of society. There may arise powers of destruction, and huge spiritual powers will be required to keep them in check. More and more, machines and automatic devices will do the physical work for humanity, and the need for spiritual play and involvement will become greater. What will people do in their free time if not create and play? People may be so in need of culture and cultural diversion that they will mine cultural treasures from ancient times. Humanity will have to exercise all its energies so as not to perish from boredom and monotony. Jewish culture, a culture of peace and of service to God, may then have even greater opportunities than it has now. Even Hasidism may have a revival in a new form as international Hasidism, of interest and significance not only for the Jews but for all peoples.

An international language, the translation of all important works into all languages, new techniques for spreading information—all this will gradually make it more and more unusual for any spiritual or cultural treasure to be the property of a single group. The Indians will know what the Chinese have created, and the Chinese will know about Hindu culture. Both will know what was and is done by Jews, Russians, and Scandinavians. In such circumstances, no culture and no artist will be isolated. Every voice that deserves to be heard will speak to the whole of humanity, and perhaps even to inhabitants of other planets. Even now, many ancient and forgotten books are being rediscovered and translated into modern languages. I believe that it will not be long before the Baal Shem and Rabbi Nahman of Bratslav may be as well known as St. Augustine or Gandhi. With the advance of modern devices of communication, it is only one step between utter oblivion and fame.

Those who love Yiddish cannot, of course, create writers and thinkers artificially, but we must apply our energies to encourage people of spirit among us. Our critics must stop praising what is raw and primitive in our writing. Our authors must get the opportunity to travel all over the world and come into contact with Jews and non-Jews. Since it is impossible to know Jewish history without knowing the history of the nations among whom the Jews have lived, a Yiddish writer must know more history than any other writer in the world.

The kind of cosmopolitanism that we must encourage should not be of the kind that strips the soul of individuality, its national roots, and then transmutes it into an instrument of communist dialectic or brainwashing. We must aspire to that kind of cosmopolitanism which is based on a deep knowledge of other people, an understanding of their essential differences, and on a religious love toward humans and animals. It was said that King Solomon knew the languages of animals and fowl, and I sincerely believe that each artist should try to follow the example of King Solomon. We will never ascend to spiritual heights if we look down on God's creatures, and if we consider them merely meat to devour, or objects of that bloody game called hunting. I believe that if there is ever to be a religious awakening and a reformulation of the old faith, it will require love and respect not only for people but also for animals—the religion of the future will include vegetarianism. How can we be sure that on the new planets which we may reach there may not be entities who regard us as animals? What would we say if creatures from Mars came to our planet, ate our meat, and murdered our children, while praying to God and writing poetry? We have much to learn from God's creatures, who many philosophers have considered nothing more than automatons.

I cannot end without mentioning psychical research, which was always a part of religion and has always been connected with art. I believe that psychical research has a great future. Someone, in fact, has said that the twenty-first century will be the century of psychical research. More and more, humanity will apply its energies to discovering the truth of its own soul. The fear of the supernatural and the bellicose skepticism of the unknown has done much damage to the advancement of science, literature, and religion. Those who deny the existence of the soul can certainly never know the soul. The laws of the soul, like the laws of nature, are still waiting to be discovered.

One thing is sure. The future will have enough practical and technical means to distribute the findings of art and science all over the world. There will be no lack of those either to receive the truth or to explore it. The main problem for each literature and each single writer is to create those works that will have value for generations to come. The masters of Yiddish, like the masters of other languages, are creating for the whole of humanity. Human culture and world literature are only at the very beginning.

Personal Writings
and Philosophy

A Trip to the Circus

Looking back on my life, I can remember always being exceedingly curious about the unusual, the mysterious, the miraculous. My father constantly spoke about saints and wonder rabbis and the miracles they worked through the power of the Kabbalah and holy names. God himself was a super miracle worker. He said, "Let there be light," and there was light. The men and women who served him, from the time of Moses to the Baal Shem Tov and Rabbi Nahman of Bratslav, were all people of magic. According to legend, those who opposed God could work magic too—Satan, Asmodeus, Lilith, all the evil hosts of demons, devils, sorcerers, as well as the builders of the Tower of Babel and the rulers of Sodom and Gomorrah.

This personal essay was written as an "Author's Note" to *The Magician of Lublin* (1960), but was never included in the novel. No Yiddish original has been found. In it, Singer gives a personal reflection on the theme of magic, including his boyhood fantasies of becoming a magician, as well as his love for Shosha, the neighbor's daughter who would serve as a muse for several stories, including a piece published in the *Forverts* as "Shoshe, di gril un der lantukh" (Shosha, the Cricket, and the Lantuch" (Oct. 3, 1967, page 2), which appeared as "Shosha" in *A Day of Pleasure: Stories of a Boy Growing up in Warsaw* (1969); and his novel *Neshome-ekspeditsyes (Soul Expeditions)*, published in the *Forverts* in 1974 and as *Shosha* in English in 1978, the year Singer was awarded the Nobel Prize for Literature.

Since my older brother Joshua tried to deny or ridicule these alleged miracles in his debates with my parents, I looked for evidence that my parents were right, not my skeptical brother. Every few days, magicians used to come to our courtyard on Krochmalna Street, and I had a chance to witness various feats of wonder. I watched them eat fire, swallow knives, stretch across boards of nails with their naked backs. A girl with flaxen blond hair, cut short like a boy's, rolled a barrel with the soles of her feet and balanced a full glass of water on a spinning wheel. My father warned me not to watch these shows, which surely contained elements of witchcraft and deception. Nevertheless, I followed these magicians from courtyard to courtyard, often giving them the groschen that I got from my mother every morning before going to *heder*. I fantasized about becoming a magician myself. I imagined that I found a cap which could make me invisible and a pair of seven league boots. I discovered a potion that made me as wise as King Solomon and as strong as Samson. Elijah would visit me at night and take me in his fiery chariot, harnessed with fiery horses, to the heavenly palaces where I would meet God, angels, seraphim, the Messiah. On the way, we would stop over in Sodom, where I could see Lot's wife, who became a pillar of salt. I also had the opportunity to enter Asmodeus's palace on Mount Seir, where the king of the netherworld sat on his throne, his black beard touching the floor, a crown of onyx stones behind his horns. Naked she-demons stood in a circle, singing blasphemous and profane songs to him.

From reading story books in Yiddish, I knew that the powers of evil were as ingenious as the powers of holiness. Even before I learned to write, I boasted to my classmates that I would write books as my father, both my grandfathers, and my brother Joshua had done.

Not only magicians were unkosher for my father, but all worldly institutions, all sciences, all arts. I heard him once say in one of his sermons that the wicked sit all day in the theater, eat pork, and fool around with salacious females. Even the gardens and public parks were taboo to him. He was told that unbelieving boys and girls in short dresses and naked arms met in these places and fell in love. To my father, love was almost as forbidden as pig meat. God-fearing young men and women only married through a matchmaker.

I realized early on that I conducted myself like a sinner. Not only did I follow the magicians from yard to yard, but I had also fallen in love with Shosha, a girl my age whose parents lived in our building. I thought about her day and night. I could not concentrate when I recited the prayers because of my yearning for her. As if all this were not enough, I used to glance into my father's books about the Kabbalah even though he warned me that a premature indulgence in its mysteries might lead to heresy and even to madness. I was terribly curious to know the secrets of Heaven and Earth. I had confided in Shosha that I was learning philosophy, astronomy, alchemy, astrology, and that I intended to run away with her and marry abroad. Shosha had given me a holy oath never to divulge my plans to anyone.

One day I had the opportunity to go secretly to the Warsaw circus with Shosha. She had an uncle who considered himself an enlightened man. He shaved his beard, wore a short jacket instead of a long gaberdine, and attended the Yiddish theater. He had bought two tickets to the circus, but a child of his fell ill and he and his wife, who did not cover her hair with a wig, had to stay home. He called my father and all Hasids fanatics. He must have had some notion of my feelings for his niece and he offered the tickets to us for nothing. Going to the circus without the knowledge of my parents, and with a girl to boot, was a tremendous adventure and a terrible risk. It was connected with many lies and other transgressions. The circus was far from our street and we had to take a trolley car by ourselves. I had to accept the carfare from her uncle, a stranger, something very forbidden in our home. I felt I was entering all the forty-nine gates of defilement and falling into an abyss of no return.

But the pleasure outweighed the sins. Shosha and I sat in the trolley car holding hands. We passed elegant streets where only non-Jews lived and we saw fancy stores with manikins dressed in splendid gowns and furs. We behaved like the lovers we read about in the Yiddish storybooks we bought for a groschen apiece. There was a chance that two unaccompanied children would not be admitted into the circus, but the powers who ruled the world decreed that the usher did not pay any attention to us. When we entered, the show had already begun. The electric lamps threw a blinding light over the stage. The orchestra was playing. We climbed up five flights of steps to the highest bench. The music was exciting beyond words. A horse was dancing to the sounds of fiddles, trumpets, cymbals, drums, and on its back stood a half-naked girl with golden hair and dazzling legs. She waved a whip and threw kisses to the applauding audience. One wonder followed another with miraculous speed. A man walked on a wire, balancing his steps with a long pole. Midgets did somersaults. A bear danced. A lion jumped through a fiery hoop. A monkey rode a bicycle. Dogs played ball. Young men and women flew like birds in midair from one trapeze to another. An elephant curled a beautiful girl inside its trunk and placed her on a golden seat on its back. A young woman jumped off a springboard and landed on the shoulders of a man.

Shosha began to scream and I could barely quiet her. All the miracles the sorcerers performed in the land of Egypt happened before my very eyes. Had I become bewitched from trying to read my father's kabbalistic books? Had I fallen into a spell of dreams and visions like the yeshiva student who bent down over a tub of water to wash his hands, and lived through all his former reincarnations in a single moment? I closed my eyes and I felt like an eagle soaring in the air through the starry night, above the roofs, over strange cities, over towers, pyramids, royal palaces, ancient fortresses, rivers, lakes, oceans, deserts, back to the time of creation, to the primeval darkness of Tohu and Bohu.

Many years had gone by, more than fifty, more than sixty. My father had died in the village where he served as a rabbi. My mother had perished in Kazakhstan, where the Russians had sent her to do forced labor. My brother had died in New York. In 1939, when the Polish radio had advised all men and able-bodied women to run from the Nazis, cross the Praga Bridge, and walk to the section of Poland that belonged to Soviet Russia, Shosha packed a satchel and took the road toward Bialystok. Along the way, she sat down to rest and never rose again. I was living in New York then, a writer in a language people considered dead. I no longer believed in God or in the powers of the Kabbalah. I had read somewhere that a self-made cosmic bomb had exploded some twenty billion years ago and that this explosion, the Big Bang, had created the universe. Since then it had been running away from itself with a constantly growing speed into the nowhere of empty space. There was no Creator, no plan, no purpose, no justice, only blind laws of nature and blind evolution. I had made up my mind that, at its best, literature was nothing more than a distraction for those trying to forget the calamity of living and dying without any hope.

Recently, a writer invited me to a literary party, and there I was introduced to a lady by the name of Paula Lipshitz, and when I asked her about her occupation—a question one never

asked a lady in former years—she told me that she was connected with the circus. "A circus?" I asked. "Do you swing on
trapezes or do somersaults on wires?" No, she answered. But
what she does is just as challenging and risky. She raises money,
she said, for a traveling circus called The Big Apple. "Doesn't
the circus maintain itself from selling tickets?" And she said,
"Not anymore. It doesn't pay a circus to travel from town to
town the way it used to in olden times. Only the children in the
very big cities have a chance to see the circus. In smaller towns
in America, years pass and they never experience the joy of see-
ing a circus unless it is shown on television. But it isn't the same.
There's a desire and a need in children as well as adults to come
into personal contact with the performer. Personal contact," she
said, "is important also in literature, in music, and even in some
sciences. Why do people attend lectures? Why do they go to
the theater instead of movies?" From the way Ms. Lipshitz
spoke, I understood that she was not only defending her job.
She was in love with The Big Apple. I had to promise her to
come see it, even though I doubted if I could still enjoy a circus
in my old age, and without Shosha.

Some weeks later, Paula Lipshitz took me out to The Big
Apple Circus, which was playing in Staten Island. The trip on
the ferry was already an enjoyable experience for me. This ferry
was my resort during my first summer in the United States. A
day did not pass when I did not spend a nickel to ride back and
forth. This ferry and the public library on Fifth Avenue were my
literary laboratories and my second home.

I stood on the deck of the ferry and fantasized about a novel
the likes of which no writer had ever written, about an environment most readers in the world had never heard of before. It
was of course written in Yiddish. This work became so famous

that the League of Nations decided to make Yiddish the international language. I had warned myself again and again not to indulge myself in these silly fantasies, which took away the best time of work. But imagining things had become a habit of mine since childhood. It was my opium. Now I stood on the ferry again, still addicted to building what they call castles in the sky.

Why I Write As I Do:
The Philosophy and Definition
of a Jewish Writer

I know in advance that anything I have to write is either known to you already or available on the shelves of your library.[1] For that reason I have decided to forget modesty and write about myself. On that subject, at any rate, I am somewhat of an authority. I hope that you will find my case history of some value.

I have in my lifetime lived through a number of epochs in Jewish history. I was brought up in a home where the old Jewish faith burned brightly. Ours was a house of Torah and holy books. Other children had toys. I played with the volumes in my father's library. I began to write before I even knew the alphabet. I took my father's pen, dipped it in ink, and started to

This essay appeared in several translated drafts, including one dated March 21, 1967, indicating it was copied from a draft dated April 10, 1962. It was published in *Esquire* as a feature titled "If You Could Ask One Question about Life, What Would the Answer Be? Yes . . . Life Is God's Novel; Help Him Write It" (Dec. 1, 1974, pages 95–96, 250, 253–54), alongside a piece by Eugène Ionesco titled ". . . No. Life Is Awful; Grimace and Bear It" (Dec. 1, 1974, pages 96, 254, 257–58). In addition, it was featured without the first paragraph as an untitled introduction to a special edition of short stories, *Gifts* (1985), which was part of The Jewish Publication Society's *Author's Workshop* series. No Yiddish original has been found.

scribble. The Sabbath was an ordeal for me because on that day writing is forbidden.

My father moved to Warsaw when I was still very young, and there a second epoch began for me: the age of the Enlightenment. My brother, I. J. Singer, who later wrote *The Brothers Ashkenazi*, was at that time a rationalist. It was not in his nature to hide his opinions. He spoke frankly to my parents, advancing with great clarity and precision all the arguments that the rationalists—from Spinoza to Max Nordau—had brought against religion. Though I was still a child, I listened attentively. Fortunately my parents did not lack answers. They replied with as much skill as my brother used to attack. I recall my father saying, "Well, who created the world? You? Who made the sky, the stars, the sun, the moon, man, the animals?" My brother's answer was that everything had evolved. He mentioned Darwin. "But," my mother wanted to know, "how can a creature with eyes, ears, lungs, and a brain evolve from earth and water?" My father used to say, "You can spatter ink, but it won't write a letter by itself." My brother never had an answer for this, and as yet none has been found.

My parents attempted to further strengthen the case for faith by constantly telling stories of imps, ghosts, and dybbuks, and of the miraculous feats of famous rabbis. They had witnessed some of these events themselves, and I knew that they were not liars. My grandfather, the Rabbi of Bilgoray, had once been visited by an old man, a fortune teller, who had been able to read the text of a closed book. Whatever page my grandfather touched with his finger—the fortune teller could recite. I later used this incident in a story of mine, "The Jew of Babylon," which has not yet been translated.[2] My mother knew of a house inhabited by a poltergeist. Indeed I can truthfully say that by the time I was seven or eight, I was already acquainted with all the strange facts that are to be found in the books of Sir Arthur Conan Doyle, Sir Oliver Lodge, Edmund Gurney and Frederic Myers, Camille Flammarion, and Professor J. B. Rhine. In our home, the most pressing questions were the eternal ones. There, the cosmic riddles were not theoretical but actual. I began to read *The Guide for the Perplexed* and the *Kuzari*, even kabbalistic literature, at an early age. But nevertheless, despite my studies, I remained a child and played joyfully with other children. At *heder*, I astounded my fellow students with fantastic stories. I told them once that my father was a king with such convincing detail that they believed me.

When the First World War broke out, I experienced all the social evils of the period. I saw the men on our street marching off to war, leaving behind them sobbing women and hungry children. Men from the very house I lived in were taken. In his debates with my brother, my father argued, "You keep on talking about reason and logic. What logic is there to this war? How does it happen that learned men and teachers assist in the manufacture of bombs and guns to destroy innocent people?" Again my brother had no answer. He himself was drafted. During the short time that he was a recruit, he endured every kind of humiliation. The Russian and Polish recruits accused him of murdering Jesus, poisoning wells, using Christian blood for matzahs, and spying for the Germans. In the barracks, reason was bankrupt. My high-minded brother fled to Warsaw and hid in the studio of a sculptor. I used to carry food to him there.

The world that was revealed to me was not rational. One could as easily question the validity of reason as the existence of God. In my own spirit, there was chaos. I suffered from morbid dreams and hallucinations. I had wildly erotic fantasies. Hungry children, filthy beggars, refugees sleeping in the streets, wagons of wounded soldiers did not arouse admiration in me for human or divine reason. The spectacle of a cat pouncing on a mouse made me sick and rebellious. Neither human reason nor God's mercy seemed to be certain. I found both filled with contradictions. My brother still clung to the hope that in the end reason would be victorious. But young as I was, I knew that the worship of reason was as idolatrous as bowing down to a graven image. I had not read the modern philosophers yet, but I had come to the conclusion by myself that reason leads to antinomies when it deals with time, space, and causality. It could deal no better with these than with the ultimate problem: the problem of evil.

In 1917, my mother took me and one of my younger brothers to Bilgoray, which was then occupied by the Austrians. Kerensky's revolution had occurred and was regarded as the victory of reason, but soon came the October Revolution and the pogroms in Ukraine. Bilgoray had just endured a cholera epidemic. The town had lost a third of its inhabitants. Some of my relatives had been stricken. The gruesome tales of that pestilence are still fresh in my memory.

Bilgoray had no railroad and was surrounded by forests, and there the Jewish traditions of a hundred years before were still very much alive. I had already become acquainted with modern Hebrew and Yiddish literature. The writers of both languages were under the influence of the Enlightenment. These authors wanted Jews to step out of their old-fashioned gaberdines and become European. Their doctrines were rationalistic, liberal, humanistic. But to me such ideas seemed already obsolete. Overthrowing one regime and replacing it with another did not seem to me to be the crux of the matter. The problem was creation itself. I felt that I must achieve some sort of solution to the puzzle or perish myself.

While in Bilgoray, I became acquainted with the literature of other nations. I read translations of Tolstoy, Dostoevsky, Gogol,

Heine, Goethe, Flaubert, Maupassant. I read Jack London's *The Call of the Wild* and the stories of Edgar Allen Poe—all in Yiddish. It was also at this time that I first studied Spinoza's *Ethics* in German translation. I pored over each page as though it were a part of the Talmud. Some of the axioms, definitions, and theorems I still remember by heart. I am now able to see the defects and gaps in Spinoza's system, but reading the *Ethics* had a great effect on me. My story "The Spinoza of Market Street" is rooted in this period. Later, I read a history of philosophy and Hume, Kant, Schopenhauer, and Nietzsche. My philosophical pursuits were not undertaken to make me a philosopher. My childish hope was to discover the truth—and through its discovery to give sense and substance to my life. But finally my conclusion was that the power of philosophy lay in its attack upon reason, not in the building of systems. None of the systems could be taken seriously. They did not help one manage one's life. The human intellect confronted existence, and existence stubbornly refused to be systematized. I myself was the insulted and shamed human intellect. Many times I contemplated suicide because of my intellectual impotence.

All these storms took place inside me. On the outside I was just a Hasidic boy who studied Gemara, prayed three times a day, and put on phylacteries. But the people of the town were suspicious anyway. They considered me an exotic plant. I saw with grief and sometimes envy how other boys my age somehow made peace with this world and its troubles. I lacked their humility.

At that time, I began to write in Hebrew. So perturbed was my spirit that I expected my pen to at least partially express my rage. But I saw with shame that nothing issued but banal and thrashed-out phrases similar to those I read in other books and which I criticized severely. I felt as if a devil or imp held onto my pen and inhibited it. A mysterious power did not let me reveal my inner self. After many trials, I decided it was the fault of the Hebrew language. Hebrew was near to me, but it was not my mother tongue. While writing, I kept on searching my memory for words and phrases from the Bible, the Mishnah, and the later literature. In addition, each Hebrew word dragged after itself a whole chain of associations. I came to the conclusion that writing in Yiddish would be easier. But I soon found that this was not so. I had still not lost my inhibitions. Satan did not allow me to express my individuality. Despite myself, I imitated Knut Hamsun, Turgenev, and even lesser writers. All creators painfully experience the chasm between their inner visions and their ultimate expression. This chasm is never completely bridged. We all have the conviction, perhaps illusory, that we have much more to say than appears on paper.

I began an investigation of the techniques of literature. What, I asked myself, makes Tolstoy and Dostoevsky so great? Is it the theme, style, or construction? My brother, I. J. Singer, had left Poland and gone to Russia. He was residing in Kiev, where he wrote for the Yiddish press, and had already published his story "Pearls." One day he showed up in Bilgoray to spend the day. As a writer, he had already "emerged." I had sufficient character not to show him my manuscripts. I knew that I had to find my way by myself.

Some time after, I went to live in Warsaw, which was then the center of Yiddish culture in Poland. It was in the early nineteen-twenties. I had not yet published anything. At that time my brother was a friend of the famous Peretz Markish, who was later liquidated by Stalin. Other members of his literary circle included Melech Ravitch, Uri Zvi Greenberg, today a famous Hebrew poet, and American Yiddish writers like Joseph Opatoshu, who came on visits to Warsaw. My brother was co-editor of the *Literarishe Bleter*, and I got a job there as a proof reader.

A spirit of revolution permeated the new Yiddish literature. Markish wrote in the style of Mayakovsky. But Alexander Blok, the Russian poet and author of the poem "Twelve," was the most beloved writer of that group. This coterie preached that classic and academic literature was bankrupt. They spoke of a new time, a new period, a new style.

I was afraid to set myself against writers who were all well recognized, though I saw that their art was new neither in spirit nor style. They had merely dressed up the old clichés in red clothing. All they did was juggle words. Even a young boy like me, from the provinces, found the doctrine that the Bolshevik Revolution would do away with all evil incredibly naive. The Jewish situation in Poland was especially bad. The Polish people—the people themselves, not merely the regime—had never come to terms with the Jews. The Jews had built a separate society in Poland, had their own faith, language, holidays, and even political aspirations. We Jews were both citizens and aliens. My father, for example, could speak no Polish. I myself spoke Polish with an accent. Though my ancestors had lived in Poland for six hundred years, we were still strangers. No revolution could unite these two communities so profoundly separated. Communism and Zionism, the two ideals which split the Jews of Poland, were both completely alien to the Polish people. I do not mean to imply by this that I had remarkable prescience, but I saw clearly that the Jews were living on a volcano. In my bitterness, I spoke about the coming catastrophe, but those around me were puffed up with optimism, rationalism, and Red dogmatism.

My brother soon freed himself of revolutionary illusions. But he still kept his belief in reason. He still thought that through evolution and progress humanity would slowly see its mistakes and correct them. We had many discussions. In a sense, I had taken over the position of my parents. I tried mercilessly to destroy his humanistic optimism. I regret now that I did this, because what did I have to offer? My parents at least advocated religion. Mine was only a negative philosophy. My brother was always tolerant and deeply sympathetic to me. But I was rebellious and often insolent.

A new *Weltanschauung* which I find difficult to characterize began to develop in me. It was a kind of religious skepticism. There is a God, but he never reveals himself. No one knows who he is or what is his purpose. There are an infinite number of universes, and even here, on this Earth, powers exist of which we have no inkling, both stronger and weaker than people. This system allowed for the possibility of angels, devils, and other beings which are and will remain forever unnamed. I had, in a curious way, combined the Ten Commandments, Humean philosophy, and the kabbalistic writing of Rabbi Moshe of Cordova and the Holy Isaac Luria, as well as the occultism of Flammarion, Sir Oliver Lodge, and Sir William Crooks. This was, as one can see, a sort of kasha of mysticism, deism, and skepticism, well suited to my intellect and temperament. Instead of a concrete universe of facts, I saw a developing universe of potentialities. The thing-in-itself is pure potential. In the beginning was potentiality. What seem to be facts are really potentialities. God is the sum of all possibility. Time is the mechanism through which potentiality achieves sequence. The Kabbalah teaches that all worlds are created through the combination of letters. My own position was that the universe is a series of countless potentialities and combinations. I had already read Schopenhauer's *The World as Will and Idea*, and knew the Schopenhauerian view that the will is the thing-in-itself, the noumenon behind the phenomenon. But to me, the basic substance of the world was potentiality seen as a whole.

I did not conceive of this as a philosophy for others, but strictly for myself. Somehow or other it made sense for me, but I didn't have the means or need to systematize it and make it understandable to others. I would say that it was more a philosophy of art than of being. God was for me an eternal belle-lettrist. His main attribute was creativity. God was creativity and what he created was made of the same stuff as he. It shared his desire: to create again. I quoted to myself that passage from the Midrash which says that God created and destroyed many worlds before creating this one. Like my brother and myself, God threw his unsuccessful works into the waste basket. The flood, the destruction of Sodom, the wanderings of the Jews in the desert, the wars of Joshua—these were all episodes in a divine novel full of suspense and adventure. Yes, God was a creator, and that which he created had a passion to create. Each atom, each molecule had creative needs and possibilities. The sun, the planets, the fixed stars, the whole cosmos seethed with creativity and creative fantasies. I could feel this turmoil within myself.

I availed myself of the doctrine of *tsimtsum*, that wonderful notion which is so important in the Kabbalah of Rabbi Isaac Luria. God, Isaac Luria says, is omnipotent, but had to diminish himself and his light so that he could create. Such shrinking is the source of creation—not only in humans but also in the Godhead. The evil host makes creation possible. God could not have his infinite works without the devil. Out of suffering, creativity is born. The existence of pain in the world can be compared to the suffering of writers describing some dreadful scene which is lived through in their imaginations. While writing, authors know that the works are only fiction produced for personal and readerly enjoyment. Each person, each animal, exists only as clay in the hands of a creator, and is itself creative. We ourselves are the writer, the book, and the character. The medieval philosophers expressed a similar idea when they said that God is himself the knower, the known, and the knowledge.

I am not seeking here to create a new philosophy. All I desire to do is to describe a state of mind. Just as artists hope throughout their whole lives to create the great and perfect work, so does God yearn throughout all eternity to perfect his creation. God is no static perfection as Spinoza thought, but a limitless and unsatiated will for perfection. All his worlds are nothing more than stages and experiments in a divine laboratory. When I went to *heder* as a boy and studied *Akdamut*, the poem for Pentecost, I was amazed by the verses which said that if all skies were parchment, all people writers, all blades of grass pens, and all the oceans ink, these would still be insufficient to describe the mysteries of the Torah. That parable became my credo: the skies were indeed parchment, the grasses pens, and all people in fact writers. Everything that existed wrote, painted, sculpted, and sought creative achievement.

Since the purpose of creation was creation, creativity was also the criterion of ethics and even of sociology. There was a place only for those social systems which could advance creativity. Freedom was nothing but the freedom to create. Since creativity required leisure, and some degree of wealth, people must create a system that would furnish the requisites necessary to experiment.

Yes, God is a writer and we are both the characters and the readers. A novel written by the Lord cannot be just for one short season. As characters in God's novel, we are all immortal. A great writer's work can be understood on many levels, and this implies that our existence has more than one meaning. We exist in body. We exist as symbols, parables, and in many other ways. When the critics praise writers they say that their characters are three-dimensional, but God's characters have more than three dimensions. Their dimensions are numberless. Good novels are often translated into many languages, and so is the novel called Life. Versions of this work are read on other planets, on other galaxies of the universe.

Apropos of the critics. Like all writers, the Almighty has his critics. We know that the angels have nothing but praise. Three times a day they sing: sublime! perfect! great! excellent! But there must be some angry critics too. They complain: Your novel, God, is too long, too cruel. Too little love. Too much sex. They advise cutting, condensing. How can a novel be good when three-fourths of it is water? They find it inconsistent, sensational, antisocial, cryptic, decadent, vulgar, pointless, melodramatic, improvised, repetitious. About one quality we all agree: God's novel has suspense. One keeps on reading it day and night. The fear of death is nothing but the fear of having to close God's book. We all want to go on with the serial forever. The belief in survival has one explanation: we refuse to have any interruptions in reading. As readers, we are burning with a desire to know the events of the next chapter, and the next, and the next. We try hard to find the formula for God's bestseller, but we are always wrong. The heavenly writer is full of surprises. All we can do is pray for a happy ending. But according to the Kabbalah, God's novel will never end. The coming of the Messiah will only be the beginning of a new volume. Resurrection will bring back some characters the reader has already forgotten, but not the writer. What we call death is but a temporary pause for purely literary reasons.

The coming of the Messiah became for me identical with the ushering in of an era when everyone would be able to create freely and search for new creative possibilities.[3]

Suddenly my way in literature became clear to me: to transform inhibition into a method of creativity, to recognize in inhibition a friendly power instead of a hostile one. In the terms of the Kabbalah, to lift up the holy sparks which had fallen from the sacred into the impure, from the World of Emanations into the unclean host. Even though I realized that this philosophy was nothing but my private concoction, I considered it valid and useful as a basis for my work. In the world of the artist, the teaching of Isaac Luria is certainly true: the shadow is often the precursor of the light, the devils and imps are temptations and challenges to further achievement. The purpose of each fall is a new rising. Each occasion for sin can become an occasion for virtue. Each passion, no matter how low, can become a ladder to ascent.

Satan in Goray, which I began writing in 1932, was a product of this state of mind. The epoch of Sabbatai Zevi was, for me, a rare opportunity to express these thoughts in a symbolic way. For me, this epoch was a lesson in both religion and creativity: one must learn from inhibition, discover its higher purpose, neither ignore it completely nor submit to it. Inhibition in the broadest sense is always an indication of new potentialities. In almost all my later works, I try to show people's urge to create, to find what is new and unique, to overcome the disturbances and barriers in their way.

Creativity is for me a very encompassing idea. I would say that everything which gives a person pleasure is creative and what causes people pain is an inhibition in their creative desire. Like Spinoza, I am a hedonist. Like the kabbalists, I believe that the male and female principles exist not only in the lower worlds but also in the higher ones. The universal novel of creation, like the novel of an earthly writer, is finally a love story.

The kabbalists compared the unclean host to the female, and this comparison has deep significance. A male can bring out his semen quickly and in abundance, but the female demands time, patience, and a period of ripening. She is, if you want, the inhibition. But she is also the power which transmutes intention into deed. The kabbalists saw in God a division into the masculine and the feminine, which they called the *Shekhinah*. God himself must have time and space for his work. In his original form, he is not perfect, but ripens in infinite time. God, like the Universe, is expanding. People can serve him by creating within their narrow worlds, in their small way, conditions that will permit creativity for all—from the bee to the human being, from the microbe that sours our milk to the greatest artist. The freedom to which we aspire should not be an end in itself. Its ultimate aim must our boundless creativity.

God creates continuously, and continuous creation is humanity's destiny too. God, like the artist, is free. Like the artist, his work cannot be predetermined. His laws are aesthetic and ethical and therefore bound to change. Continual change is their very essence. Beauty is their purpose. God's fantasy is their limit. God, like the artist, never knows clearly what he will do and how his work will develop. Only the intention is clear: to bring out a masterpiece and to improve it all the time. I once called God a struggling artist. This continual aspiration is what people call suffering. In this system, emotions are not passive as in Spinoza's philosophy. God himself is emotion. God thinks and feels. Compassion and beauty are two of his endless attributes. The Kabbalah reveals only ten *sefirot* or attributes. We may add as many as our imagination can see. In my novel *The Slave*, I have expressed this notion in these words:[4]

The summer night throbbed with joy. From all sides came music. Warm winds bore the smells of grain, fruit, and pine trees to him. Itself a kabbalistic book, the night was crowded with sacred names and symbols—mystery upon mystery. In the distance, where sky and earth merged, lightning flashed, but no thunder followed. The stars looked like letters of the alphabet, vowel points, notes of music. Sparks flickered above the bare furrows. The world was a parchment scrawled with words and song. Every now and then Jacob heard a murmur in his ear as if some unseen being was whispering to him. He was surrounded by powers, some good, some evil, some cruel, some merciful, but each with its own nature and its own task to perform.[5]

A Personal Concept of Religion

People often ask me: Are you religious? And it isn't easy for me to answer because the basic element of religion is divine revelation, whether God reveals himself in a burning bush or through the intervention of an angel. But can there also be a religion that does not rely upon revelation?

The fact is that a number of philosophers preached this very kind of religion, but the God of philosophers never could

This essay was first published in the *Forverts* under the name Varshavski in three installments—"A perzenlikhe oyffasung fun religie" (A Personal Conception of Religion, August 9, 1966, page 4), "Di getlikhe kunst un dos getlikhe visn" (Divine Art and Divine Knowledge, Aug. 10, 1966, page 4), and "Mayn bagrif vegn got un di flikhtn fun mentsh" (My Concept of God and the Duties of Man, Aug. 11, 1966, page 2). It was presented as part of a lecture series on "The Writer at Work" organized by the Gallatin Division of New York University, excerpts of which appeared in *The New York Times* under the title "What Is God to Do—Discuss His Book with Every Reader?" (section A, page 29). It was also the 1980 Flora Levy Lecture in the Humanities at the University of Southern Louisiana, where it was printed in a ten-page pamphlet under the title "My Personal Conception of Religion." The version included here, which includes the alternative title "Religion Without Dogma," appears to be a later draft, since it includes the crossing out of sections that appear in the published pamphlet. In his earlier essay, "Why I Write As I Do," Singer conceived of the Godhead as a novelist. In this essay, he reformulates the Godhead as an artist, openly admitting to fashioning his idea of God after himself. This premise allows him to expand on the ideas of the earlier essay, and describe the expression of divinity in the world as a drama of creativity.

acquire prophets, temples, or priests. To the best of my knowledge, there is no temple where people pray to Spinoza's Substance,[1] or Hegel's Zeitgeist. When people serve God, it is a God who speaks to them, issues commands, hears prayers and rewards them—in this life, or after death. It is no coincidence that all religions have portrayed God as a king. Just like a king, a human being's God must reward richly and punish severely. Like a king, he must possess treasures and have his favorites and his traitors. No matter how awesome Nature may appear to us, we will neither pray to it nor sacrifice ourselves on her behalf.

If religion must be closely bound with revelation, then I cannot properly call myself a religious person.[2] But, at the same time, I believe—without revelation—that there is a God who rules the world and keeps watch over us. I often pray to this God although I have no clear conception of what he is, what his demands are, nor what his aims and motives are.

I have made peace with the concept that it is possible—at least for me—to serve a God who is silent. At the same time, my God is not Spinoza's indifferent Nature, but a God with all the divine attributes. Spinoza's God lacks will, purpose, or compassion. For him there is no good or evil. He has no will, purpose, sense of justice.[3] But I have built for myself a private God.[4] I've endowed my God with all the properties and attributes that appeal to me. I've fashioned him precisely to suit my taste. I formed him out of my intellect, my emotions, my limited experience.[5] Do not suggest to me that he is a product of my imagination, since I freely concede this, nor accuse me of stealing my concept from others. I confess that I borrowed whatever I liked. Mine is an eclectic God.

Along with Jews, Christians, and all other religious philosophers, I believe that God has existed forever. I can no more picture the birth or death of God than I can conceive of the beginning or end of time, or the limit of space.

I can easily make peace with Spinoza's contention that God is identical with Nature. But I do not agree that God is a rigid mechanism, a slave of his own laws. My God must be dynamic, creative, possessed of boundless fantasy and infinite wisdom. I despise cruelty in people, and I could not permit the thought that my God can be cruel. He must combine wisdom with goodness. I love beauty in works of art, and my God must possess beauty.

I do not care for people or works of art that lack love. My God must be a lover—eternally in love. But with whom can he be in love? My answer is: with his creations. Here I am prepared to draw on the Kabbalah. The kabbalists saw in God the principle of male and female. According to the kabbalists, the higher spheres abound in unions. Angels, seraphim, cherubim, and holy souls are engaged in divine loves. God himself bears a godly love toward the Divine Presence, the *Shekhinah*. But like all lovers, he has his obstacles. In the text of the hymn *Akdamut*, it states that God creates a batch of new angels daily. It is possible that he creates them to satisfy his craving for love. Love and creation are to God one and the same thing.

Every artist is an experimenter, and my God experiments eternally. His every star, every planet is an experiment, a part of the divine laboratory. True art is not chaotic, and God's works are the opposite of chaos. In other words, if he is an artist, he is not a modernist.

No work of art can consist entirely of light and positivism. In every genuine work of art there should be light and shade, harmony and disharmony. True artists do not give away all their secrets at the very beginning. Often the artists themselves don't know precisely in which direction their pens or brushes are heading. They often surprise themselves.

My God boasts all the artistic qualities. He creates and he fails. He makes artistic errors, then corrects them. He creates the most varied and unexpected situations. Since he is unlimited as to quantity and quality, he has used up only a minuscule part of his power and originality. He is not the fixed mechanism of the materialists, but a God who evolves and forever changes his form and direction. New ideas constantly ferment within him. He is full of divine emotions. He wages a struggle against innumerable inhibitions.

Did he, himself, create these inhibitions? Are they a part of his nature? I do not believe in an absolute perfection. God keeps on improving himself. He is mighty, but not so almighty that he need no longer struggle. Godliness is struggle. His entire existence is one crisis. He and his creation stand in constant danger. God is eternally fearful of exhausting his divine powers, falling into the web of routine.[6] He must maintain an eternal watch over himself.

He is full of restfulness, but also seethes with unrest. He is pleased by his achievements, but grieved by his failures. Some of his works must be done over. Some of his experiments may lead into a blind alley. It is true that he has sufficient time and space to correct matters, but[7] he has undertaken so many plans and tasks that one eternity is insufficient for him. He must create new eternities. He is not only the painter, he must also provide the canvas. He is not merely the playwright, he must also put up the theater and construct the stage.

My God is not only an artist, he is a scientist as well. In God, art and science are one and the same. Artists and scientists must have their disciples. God is not a writer who writes for the drawer, nor an inventor who creates toys for himself. God must have his public. He welcomes judgment. He is not afraid of adverse criticism, but he cannot make his efforts too obvious. His creations must have tension. What's more, even an artist such as he need not please everyone equally.

There are those readers who protest: He is no writer at all. They maintain that His works lack rhyme or reason. He doesn't even exist! A cosmic inkwell exploded and a universal chaos resulted. But what is God to do—discuss his books with every reader? Reveal chapters that are scheduled to come later? Present the third act before the second? God doesn't give interviews, nor does he answer questions that might occur to his readers.[8] He is above locking himself up in an ivory tower, but his silence is just as imperative as his speech.

God does reveal himself, but gradually—line by line. He demands the reader's trust, but if the reader refuses to trust him and becomes impatient, he cannot help him.[9]

The greatest misunderstanding rampant among God's readers is in their concept of death. Nearly all of them are convinced that when a chapter ends, so does the novel. But to allow the readers to remember all the chapters is impossible. God's novel is too long to be recorded in a single brain, in a single life. The readers must change along with the situations, since in God's novel, they are also his characters, as in his theater, the spectators are also the actors.

Actors cannot remain constantly onstage. They must play their parts, then retire into the wings. They must change their costumes and their makeup for new roles. The old parts aren't lost. Every word, every sound is recorded. In God's theater, in God's library, in God's museum, nothing is ever lost. If he chooses, he can play everything over again. To God, the resurrection of the dead is an easy task. Plays that have ended in one theater are often restaged in other theaters. Everything that has lived, lives on forever.

All problems concerning God can be reduced to a single question: Why the suffering? The answer is: Without suffering there is no art. Suffering and joy represent the elements of the divine drama. God, the Creator, is himself the Universal Sufferer. Our suffering is his suffering. We are he. Whoever arrives at this truth can accept suffering with some patience. Good readers don't become angry with their favorite authors when some situation displeases them.

The questions is: What are your responsibilities to such a God? How do you serve a God who seems to ignore you completely?

My answer is as personal as my concept of God.[10] No matter how small our role in the world drama, we do participate in it.[11] We are granted a measure of free choice.[12] We can play our role truthfully or falsely. I do not agree with Spinoza that everything is completely determined, that we behave in a pattern prescribed since eternity. I choose to believe the opposite: God is free and he delegates freedom to his creatures. Freedom is to me a divine attribute. Human freedom is part of divine freedom. Yes, in a sense, we ourselves write or edit our own role.

Even if God did not reveal himself, the Ten Commandments are the nearest thing to truth, justice, and even beauty, as far as I am concerned. Their principle is that one's happiness should not be based on the misery of others.[13] I cannot imagine a religion founded on the opposite principle. I personally apply this principle not only to people, but to *all* of God's creatures. I do not want to satisfy my appetite on the misery of a steer or a chicken. As long as these creatures are not granted their rights, all faiths remain unjust.

The Ten Commandments state a principle, but not the method of realizing it. The fact is that often this principle appears impossible to achieve. For thousands of years, humanity has preached peace, but wars go on. The streets are overrun with murderers, swindlers, and thieves. But I still say to myself: this is the only way.[14] If I am wrong, and God prefers murder, theft, and falsehood, I would rather serve an idol of justice than a God of injustice.

For me it is no longer a question of whether or not the Ten Commandments are right, but how they can best be applied in every relationship between person and person, humans and beasts, men and women.[15] Since the Ten Commandments are based on a free choice between good and evil, I must accept free choice as a reality, not as an illusion.[16] I do not feel obliged to accept such religious dogmas as the sacrifice of animals, wearing ritual fringes, or putting on phylacteries. Some of these dogmas have been, and could continue to remain, useful as symbols that remind people of their responsibilities. But to me, they are interchangeable with other dogmas.

On the other hand, the service of God must be bound up with discipline. One cannot simply read the Ten Commandments and agree with them. Our entire life is filled with temptations to break the Ten Commandments. It requires an iron will to go through life according to their teachings.[17] The Torah is to me a guidebook by which we learn how to play our role to the best of our ability. Since the drama keeps constantly changing, with new roles and new characters ever unfolding, the Torah cannot remain static.

I believe in a dialectical approach to dogma. It is the tragedy of all religions that dogmas have supplanted principles—that the means have become an end.[18] Actually, dogma is only as valuable as its contribution to the moral and spiritual elevation of humanity, to a sense of justice and compassion for all that lives, and to a dedication to the great enigma we call God.[19] My God is one who goes forward. I almost said he is a Godseeker. Yes, God searches within his boundless potentials. He is free.[20] However, after the first chapter of a novel has been written, writers are no longer completely free. They have created characters that cannot be overlooked in subsequent chapters.[21]

Even though God and people find themselves in constant crisis, I am confident that in never-ending time, everything will turn out better than the human imagination could ever conceive. Paradise and the resurrection of the dead are symbols of the great goodness and beauty which the Master Artist is capable of creating. He can repay many times over for our suffering and his. He has reserves of great joy. Happiness is not exclusively a human pursuit. God, too, strives for happiness.

Since God lives and everything that exists emanates from him, there is no such thing as death. Death is a temporary institution.[22] That which we call death is the constant change of form, the eternal ascent from grade to grade.

My faith is not such that I could try to impose it upon others. It is a personal faith, born of my fantasy and my dreams. Its basis is tolerance. How can one be intolerant when one has no revelations to back up one's beliefs?

Since my religion consists of seeking God, rather than serving one already found, I am an adherent of what is called psychical research. Each fact, no matter how strange, should be investigated. God has countless surprises for us. Science in general, and psychical research in particular, will encounter experiences which people today would have considered absurd.

Creation has neither end, nor limit, nor quality and quantity.[23] Every part of creation is endless. Since we ourselves are parts of this eternity, we can always discover something new and unique. Human beings are, by their very nature, discoverers, inventors, and creators. They are, because of this, the very image of God.[24]

If it doesn't serve any other purpose, this personal point of view will help, I hope, to clarify the way of thinking of a single writer.

A Story about a Collection
of Stories

Since I am supposed to be a "born storyteller," as one of my
lenient critics called me, the introduction to this collection will
contain two little stories. One facetious and one true. The first
one is that when I was born my mother asked the midwife, "Is
it a boy or a girl?" And the midwife answered, "A writer." I have
told this anecdote to so many people so many times that I am
beginning to believe that it is true. This "event" took place, as
you may know, in 1903.[1]

The other one happened about twenty-five years later. I was
already known in the Yiddish Writers' Club in Warsaw as a
promising young short story writer. The most important Yiddish
publisher, Boris Kletzkin, offered to publish a collection of my
stories. This was an unbelievable stroke of luck for a fledgling
writer, and many of my colleagues envied me. I promptly delivered the manuscript to my publisher and it was set in type, actually in hand-type, which took quite a long time. I had stipulated
in my contract that the first proofs should be read by a proof-
reader and the second proofs by myself. One morning I received
the second proofs and began to read them. I read them late into

This short piece appeared as an introduction to a Franklin Library edition of
Gimpel the Fool and Other Stories (1983). The single English draft is dated February 7,
1979. No Yiddish original has been found.

the night. The longer I read them, the less I liked them. In the beginning, I thought I could correct these stories, even though elaborate changes meant a great deal of time, effort, and money. After long brooding I came to the conclusion that no changes would make this collection please me. There was only one way out, to give up the whole thing. I knew that when my publisher heard about my decision, he would be flabbergasted. He would also be entitled to collect his costs from me, but I could not spare a single groschen from my meager earnings. It was a terrible night for me, but I was ready for any sacrifice. Anything was better than to come out with a collection of stories I disliked.

The next day, when I told my decision to my publisher, he fell into a rage. He had liked my short stories. He even went so far as to advertise them. He called me the vilest names. And since I made a living from doing translations from German, Polish, and sometimes Hebrew for this very publisher, I knew I was out of a job as well. After much haggling, my publisher insisting that the writing was good and my telling him that what I wrote was bad, we decided not to publish the book. As compensation for his losses, I was to translate two books for him without any pay. I was more than willing. I had saved both my job and my name as a writer. I remember promising the publisher that not later than two years hence I would bring him a new manuscript.

About five years later I went to America without having published the promised collection. As a matter of fact, I didn't wait five years, but twenty-seven years until I came out with a collection of short stories—in English translation, not in the original Yiddish. This book, *Gimpel the Fool and Other Stories*, is my first collection of stories. The Yiddish version came out under the title *Gimpel tam un andere dertseylungen* about five years later. The proofs of the collection I rejected I still have somewhere among my papers. It was a hard decision to make but I was

brought up to believe that literature must have enduring qualities, not to be published for one season and fade out into the
entropy of cheap paperbacks.

I dedicate this collection to Boris Kletzkin, who never made a
penny from publishing. The very opposite, he lost all his fortune
in it. The two books which I translated for him were Knut Hamsun's *Victoria* and *Pan*. Of course I didn't know Norwegian. I used
the German, Polish, and Hebrew translations of these works. I
promise The Franklin Library not to pull the same trick on them.
I could hardly afford to wait another twenty-seven years.

The Making of a First Book

From the day people could think, they dreamed of powers that would adjust the natural order of things to their desires and caprices. Among humanity's greatest victories was the discovery of fire. What a miracle it was that rubbing two sticks together could light up the night, roast and cook meat, bring warmth into the cave, and frighten vicious beasts! Some imagined that human willpower in itself would work even greater miracles. Long before people discovered fire, they knew that an act of love was creative and that hatred was destructive.

The Jews who brought to the world the belief in one God—the Creator of Heaven and Earth—never denied the power of magic, demons, sorcery. Magic was a tool for humanity's exploration of its own hidden forces. The book of Exodus tells us that with their enchantments, the sorcerers in Egypt accomplished

This essay first appeared in English as an introduction to a special edition of *Satan in Goray* published by Sweetwater editions in 1981, which included etchings by Ira Moskowitz. While summarizing some of his earlier writing on Kabbalah, Singer here shows how they were exploited in the seventeenth century by the false messiah Sabbatai Zevi, putting them into historical context. Singer gives these themes and events a personal treatment, tracing how they were harnessed in the composition of his first novel—which first appeared serially in Warsaw in 1933 and in book form in 1935, the year Singer left Poland and emigrated to the United States. The book was reprinted in Yiddish in the United States in 1943 and appeared in English translation in 1955, over twenty years after it was first published. No Yiddish original of this essay has been found.

almost as much as Moses and Aaron. In the book of Samuel, we learn that when King Saul suffered defeat in his wars, he went to a witch in Endor, and she called the spirit of the prophet Samuel to appear before him. Jewish mysticism is as old as, or perhaps much older than, monotheism. The idea that Judaism is a religion of rationality is false. In times of sickness, famine, and other misfortunes, all people are drawn to what we call superstition or fanaticism. Two thousand years of exile and persecution tempted Jews to investigate the mystical powers. They believed in angels, devils, witches, and in the validity of incantations and amulets. Little was written down about Jewish mysticism until the thirteenth century, when Rabbi Moshe de León published the *Zohar*. Until then the lore of the Kabbalah was passed down orally. Travelers who raised funds for the poor as well as for the maintenance of yeshivas and sacred graves in the Holy Land came to the lands of the Diaspora and brought tidings of kabbalistic revelations. They told fantastic stories about the Wailing Wall where the Holy Presence still lingered—and of souls hovering over ancient hills, rocks, and graves. Angels, seraphim, cherubim, and *arelim* soared in the sky above Jerusalem, while in the ruins of Sodom and Gomorrah, Satan, Asmodeus, and their evil females—Lilith, Naama, and Mahlat—still fought for the dominion of the Netherworld. God was still God and the Jews remained his chosen people. Any day the prophet Elijah was bound to blast the ram's horn of the Messiah and announce that the redemption had come. High above the constellations, a fiery Holy Temple was being formed, ready to descend to Jerusalem at the appointed time. From the sandy graves of the Mount of Olives would emerge the first saints in the miracle of resurrection.

The Talmudists considered delving into the mysteries of creation a most dangerous venture. Heresy or insanity could be the result. Just the same, Jewish mysticism continued to develop and influence mystics of other faiths—and be influenced by them. The Kabbalah, which means "receiving," was the name for Jewish mysticism. It was believed that the Jews received their mystical truths on Mt. Sinai and that the Torah, as we know it, was only an outer garment to those mysteries and truths—if one made an effort to unravel them. To achieve this kind of knowledge all forms of asceticism and prayer were practiced on a grand scale—combining letters and numbers, acts of meditation, fasting and immersion in ritual baths. True, in their prayers, Jews addressed themselves to God alone, to the highest authority in the heavenly hierarchy. Jews could never allow themselves to believe that flesh and blood, no matter how great and divine, could have the power of God, or that God could refuse to listen to the supplications of the sufferers directly. But one must also recognize the sacred powers of His Retinue on High.

Just as the thirteenth century reactivated the Jewish spirit with the appearance of the *Zohar*, the sixteenth century brought the version of the Kabbalah of Isaac Luria and of his disciple Rabbi Chaim Vital to unmeasurable heights. Rabbi Isaac Luria had not only created a new style of the Kabbalah, as did Rabbi Moshe of Cordova, but he made the Kabbalah the foundation of Jewish faith and hope all over the world. Paradoxically, Rabbi Isaac Luria broadened the horizons of the Kabbalah by bringing into it the idea of divine shrinking—that in order to be able to create a world, all worlds, the Infinite One had to shrink his eternal power, conceal his face, dim his radiance, and thus form a vacuum within himself. This vacuum became the condition and the background for godly and later human creativity. Before God said, "Let there be light," he had to make place for darkness, the "Tohu and Bohu" into which he sent a beam of his light. To be able to create the world, God needed to establish an opposition to himself, a negative which would be the basis of the positive. Without it, his light would have dazzled all his works. Without the existence of evil, God could not bring out the crown of his creativity—humankind—and the gift of free choice bestowed upon him. Humans, the weakest link in the chain of Emanation, are actually the cornerstone of divine evolution. When people succeed, God succeeds. Our failure does damage to all spheres.

It is characteristic of every kind of mysticism that it is connected to the mysteries of sex. According to the Kabbalah, the Jewish exile was linked to a heavenly sexual crisis. When the Jews sinned they caused God to separate himself from the *Shekhinah*—his feminine aspect. True unity between God and the *Shekhinah* could only take place when the Jews repented their transgressions, returning to God and his Torah. God, Jews, and the Torah are one, the *Zohar* tells us. The suffering of the Jews is God's suffering. However, without suffering, free choice is impossible. The secrets and riddles of the Jewish soul are identical to the secrets and riddles that are found in the Torah and in acts of providence. The sexual act is called "knowledge" in the book of Genesis. The loving copulation of male and female is an act of knowledge. Kindred souls yearn one for the other and desire to merge. The body itself is made of a spiritual substance. The passions of the flesh are the passions of the soul: a thirst and a curiosity which can never be completely quenched—a satisfaction which can grow stronger and invigorate the universal potency.

In a way, the Jewish exile is the exile of the human species according to the Kabbalah. The souls of all people have lost themselves in hatred, wars, envy, and pettiness—but try constantly to find themselves. Smaller souls long to attach themselves to higher souls. The eternal Eve lusts for the eternal

Adam. Divine lights must find vessels through which they can enter and enrich one another. The flow of spiritual essence is sometimes so great that it breaks these vessels and godly substance is spilled into an abyss from which it must sooner or later be recovered.

Sexual desire can be both a source of great delight and a dangerous temptation. The first chapters in the book of Genesis describe the relation between male and female as a kind of celestial risk. God made Adam fall asleep when he formed Eve from his rib. Soon after that Adam and Eve realized that something was wrong with their corporeal image, and being ashamed of it they tried to cover it. The principle of all mysticism is expressed in the first chapter of the Bible. Something is overly strong and overly fragile in the relation of sex. It is always on the brink of both the highest achievement and of the deepest fall. The vulnerability of humankind is the vulnerability of life and the whole of creation, which the kabbalists saw as a kind of Godly experiment, with the Jew as the catalyst in God's chemistry.

There are no clear dates for the arrival of the first Jews in Poland, but the track seems to lead from Spain into Germany and from there to Poland. The exile from Spain, the persecution which the Jews suffered in Germany as well as in France and England, along with their arrival into a country which was not totally divested of paganism, must have deeply affected these Jewish wanderers. Along with an adjustment to this new climate, there emerged new hopes and a new sense of mystery in these people. They had left many material treasures in the countries from which they had been driven out—yet they brought with themselves not only the Bible and the books of the Talmud, but also the *Zohar*, *The Book of Creation*, and other kabbalistic works.

There was no danger of assimilation for the Jews in Poland because the Poles had not yet managed to develop a mature culture of their own. In Poland, it was easier for the Jews to remain in contact with Jews in the Holy Land, where the Kabbalah blossomed. In the Holy Land, many kabbalists and ascetics settled in caves or tents near ancient graves, making calculations and attempting to decipher the End of Days by reading obscure passages in the book of Daniel and other holy texts. Some of these kabbalists were influenced by the ideas of the gnostics, by Plato, Pluto, Philo of Alexandria, and even by Arabic religious thinkers.

It often happened in Jewish history that great events—great processes of Jewish creativity—went hand in hand with terrible catastrophes. The Mishnah and the Gemara would have not become what they are without the destruction of the Second Temple, without the Diaspora. The *Zohar* preceded the calamity of the Jewish exile from Spain. The catastrophe of Bohdan Khmelnytsky came after Rabbi Isaac Luria managed to imbue Judaism with new and sublime spiritual values. And soon after came the turmoil of the Sabbatai Zevi era. The terrible slaughter of Polish Jews during the rebellion of Khmelnytsky's Cossacks was of such blind cruelty that it must have shocked the faith of Jews all over the world. Never before and never after did the Jews serve God and follow the Torah with such zeal as in the time of this calamity. The Torah and its commandments were virtually the air the Polish Jews breathed. Many Jews felt that this mighty blow could not have been just a punishment for some minor transgressions or an act of temptation. There was only one explanation for this national debacle—the birth throes of the Messiah.

The Sabbatai Zevi movement came so close to the Khmelnytsky disaster that one might as well say they happened simultaneously. The truth is that the Kabbalah generally, and Isaac Luria's version of the Kabbalah especially, in a way enhanced the Sabbatai Zevi hysteria. After some fifteen hundred years of studying about what was kosher and what was *treyf*, what was permitted and what was forbidden, the people had developed a yearning for something higher, for some lore rich in collective imagination, for promises that would enliven and invigorate the battered Jewish spirit. Sabbatai Zevi never tried to deny the validity of the Talmud and its commentaries. Just the same, in his indoctrination he made more and more use of Kabbalah rather than of *Halakhah*, which constantly accentuated what the Jews owed to the Almighty, while rarely mentioning that the Almighty owed something to the Jews, whose history was one unbroken series of martyrdoms for his name. True, the Talmudists promised the pious Jews paradise, but so many laws and bylaws were added by the rabbis that almost no one could keep them all. Sooner or later even the most devout were bound to suffer punishment in Gehenna for negligence or mistakes in their conduct or for their false interpretation of the law. The writers of the Talmudic laws elaborated on the various chastisements that those who break them should expect, but the quality of the reward for keeping them was seldom discussed.

The Kabbalah did the opposite. The very fact that the Kabbalah divided the attributes of God into those of mercy and judgment constituted, in a way, a reproach to the scholars who clung to the vigor of the law. The books of *muser*, or morality, constantly pointed out the dangers that lurk around all of us—and how easy it is to lose the world to come. But the Kabbalah accentuated God's light. His grace. His compassion. According to the kabbalists, even the harshness of the law constituted masked clemency. Even Satan and his devils were not all evil. In the Kabbalah, transgressions did not appear as dismal as in the books of the *Halakhah*, the codes of law. Because the Kabbalah was and remained thoroughly pantheistic, there was no room for absolute godlessness. If all worlds were emanations of the Godhead, everything had to be rooted in the sublime. The kabbalistic idea that copulations of male and female take place not only on Earth but also in the mansions of Heaven lifted the spirit of the Jews who studied the Kabbalah. It promised them sacred pleasures and gave a different status to the female, who was for the *Halakhah* not much more than an object of temptation and a pitfall of sin. The Kabbalah had brought eroticism into Jewishness. It was not a mere accident that all objects in the Hebrew language and in many other languages were divided into masculine and feminine. The principle of male and female existed in the deepest abyss and in the highest spheres of Godliness. The kabbalists hoped and prayed for a reunion between God and the *Shekhinah*. God and the *Shekhinah* were father and mother to all beings. Their separation was a cause of cosmic mourning, their reunion a solace for all.

Had the Sabbatai Zevi movement remained within the teachings of the Kabbalah, it would never have evoked such terrible opposition from the rabbis and other Jewish leaders as it did. But Sabbatai Zevi and his disciples went even further in their opposition to *Halakhah* than did the early Christians. They founded their perverted religious outlook on a saying in the Gemara that the Messiah will come to a generation that is either completely virtuous or completely guilty. And since the chances of having a generation that is completely virtuous are always very small, they aimed at bringing into being a generation that would be completely guilty. They maintained that redemption cannot come without the help of Satan and his host. The only way to bring the Messiah was by indulging more and more in deeds of iniquity. There were few Jews who were tempted to eat pork, or leavened bread on Passover, or to serve idols. The Jewish soul certainly did not yearn for murder. But many were tempted to commit sins of an erotic nature because of the severe restrictions the rabbis had added generation after generation. The *Halakhah* had tried to curb the sexual desire of the Jew. A pious Jewish man was not allowed to look at a woman who was not his wife. He was told to perform the sexual act as if forced by a demon. He was not permitted to enjoy his passion, but to live with his wife only for the sake of fulfilling the commandment: to be fruitful and multiply. The Song of Songs was interpreted by the Talmudist as a dialogue between God and the congregation of Israel. In this respect, the scholars of *Halakhah* resembled the Christian theologians who could not make peace with the idea that the Bible contained a love poem without any religious significance. Love in the Bible could only mean love of God.

The idea that sin might help bring the Messiah must have appealed to many Jews, young and old. Some scholars discovered a saying that a number of the Torah's commandments, among them the prohibition of incest, might be changed in the Messianic times. Many kabbalistic scholars maintained that in the higher spheres, males and females indulged in celestial intercourse. Jacob continued to copulate with the sisters Rachel and Leah, as well as with his concubines Bilhah and Zilpah. These kabbalists maintained that sensuality reaches as high as the Throne of Glory. The Kabbalah taught its own system of relativity. What is wrong in one sphere and in one time may be right in another sphere and another time. It was known that Sabbatai Zevi married a former prostitute from Rome named Sarah. According to Sabbatai Zevi, he had been bidden to marry a harlot, as was the prophet Hosea. It says in the Talmud that if a man repents, his sins turn into good deeds. The very fact that a sin could become a good deed meant that there is a nucleus of good and higher purpose even in sinning. Sabbatai Zevi and his prophets were masters of casuistry—twisting the text of the Bible, the Midrash, the Mishnah, and the Gemara to fit their distorted sense of Judaism. Some of them were even inclined to find support for their statements in the New Testament and in the works of the Gnostics. Prophets arose who not only proclaimed Sabbatai Zevi as the true Messiah, but even called him God. Sabbatai Zevi himself had reached this degree of megalomania. It is known that from the time the Jews had been driven out from their land, no one was allowed to pronounce the name of Yahweh as it is written. This privilege was granted to the high priest only on the day of Yom Kippur when he entered the Holy of Holies. It was thought that when the Messiah came he might pronounce this name even before the Temple would be rebuilt. One day in the year 1648, Sabbatai Zevi entered the synagogue in the Turkish city of Izmir and uttered this supernal name before the whole assembly. The very fact that a man dared to go so far was considered by his worshippers to be proof that he was the true redeemer.

An even greater proof to them was the fact that the sultan did not punish Sabbatai Zevi the way he normally would have punished someone who tried to proclaim himself the Messiah, the coming ruler of the Holy Land, the King of Israel. When the sultan's lords, like the grand vizier, finally convinced the sultan that Sabbatai Zevi acted like a traitor and a rebel to his crown, the sultan did not send Sabbatai Zevi to the gallows, as he would have done in a similar case. He put him instead into large quarters in a fortress with the freedom to receive venerable visitors. Sabbatai Zevi was supposed to live there like some pasha or caliph who had displeased the sultan in a small way. He was surrounded by great lords, ambassadors, and scholars who came to hear his words of wisdom and his revelation of heavenly mysteries. The disciples of Sabbatai Zevi spread the news that their leader had taken over the power of the sultan by supernatural means.

It is a historical fact now that not only Jews, but Muslims and Christians fell under the influence of Sabbatai Zevi and his teachings. These Christians expected the redemption of the Jews to come simultaneously with the Second Coming of Jesus. More and more Jews in Germany, Holland, and Poland—among them religious leaders—began to believe that God had finally sent his Messiah to his chosen people of Israel. Many Jews all over the world were tired of living with constant promises and without any sign of fulfillment. There was a great yearning among them for freedom from oppression and for a return to the Land of Israel.

It is not an exaggeration to say that in some way the tidings of Sabbatai Zevi were early precursors of Zionism. More than that, Sabbatai Zevi's belief in the power of eroticism in some way presaged the Freudianism of our epoch. It also contained some elements of Hasidism, which came a hundred years later and preached religion through joy. It is noteworthy that the opponents of the Hasidim—the Misnagdim—nicknamed the Hasidim "Sabbatai Zeviniks." Paradoxical as it may sound, even the *Haskalah*, the Jewish Enlightenment, which was all rationalism, had roots in the Sabbatai Zevi movement. The followers of Sabbatai Zevi wanted to get rid of the multitude of dogmas with which the Jews burdened themselves in the generations of utter isolation from worldliness. The followers of Sabbatai Zevi were mystical hedonists. Their main belief was that man can serve God best by discovering all the possible variations of pleasure. Many mystics before and after felt that the human soul was a goldmine of bliss—of intellectual and emotional treasures that had to be dug out and brought to the surface. The Kabbalah teaches us that God is the source of all joy and that there is a kind of religious magic by which people can reach its depths. Humanity has been, is, and will always be a seeker of pleasure—whether it is to be found here or in the hereafter.

I find it necessary to say a few words about myself. I was brought up in a house which, I might say, was a reliving of Jewish history in a miniature way. The Bible, the Mishnah, the Talmud, the *Zohar*, and all the Jewish movements were as real in our house as if they happened on Krochmalna Street where my father lived and served as a rabbi. The patriarchs Abraham, Isaac, and Jacob were not just distant ancestors for us, but real grandparents. Every event told in the book of Genesis was more tangible in our home than the news we read in the Yiddish daily newspaper. My mother was my Bible teacher. My father taught me the Mishnah and the Talmud and constantly warned me against studying the Kabbalah prematurely—before the age of thirty. This made me want to study it immediately.

Hundreds and even thousands of years seemed as near to us as yesterday. I was seriously in love with Mother Rachel even before I fell in love with our neighbor's daughter Shosha. The Khmelnytsky holocaust was closer to me than the pogroms in Russia or Romania. There was not a day when my father did not discuss Sabbatai Zevi, Jacob Frank, the Baal Shem, the Vilna Gaon. The controversy between Rabbi Jonathan Eybeschutz and Rabbi Jacob Emden in the eighteenth century seemed to have taken place right before my eyes. My grandfather, the Rabbi of Bilgoray, sided with Rabbi Jacob Emden, while my father sided with Rabbi Jonathan. Often my mother tried to make peace between her father, who lived far away in Bilgoray, and her husband. I, their little son, agreed with Rabbi Jonathan and considered grandfather a zealot. Rabbi Emden had accused Rabbi Jonathan of being a secret follower of Sabbatai Zevi—of giving out talismans where the name of Sabbatai Zevi was inscribed either fully or symbolically. Rabbi Jonathan denied it, of course, because Sabbatai Zevi's disciples were all excommunicated. This quarrel had taken place some two hundred years earlier, but as far as I was concerned it happened only yesterday.

When I began to write, my pen took me back to all these youthful experiences. Most of the Yiddish writers of the time described life in the *shtetl*: the rich man, the poor man, the yeshiva boy who fell in love with a wealthy girl. It was all mildly romantic, sentimental, on the side of positivism and the already obsolete Enlightenment. I felt that most of those writers had overlooked the great passions and disappointments of humanity generally and of the Jewish condition specifically. I knew that the history and the spirit of the Jews is infinitely richer than what these writers were describing.

I remember reading a story by Sholem Aleichem, whom I admired highly, about a boy who wanted to study in a Russian gymnasium and wasn't allowed because of his Jewishness. I thought, "Is this the Jewish tragedy, that they don't let a boy study in some Russian school? Is petty and partial assimilation the answer to our two-thousand-year-old martyrdom?" Many of the Jewish writers seemed consumed with fighting the antisemites. In the process of defending Jews and trying to show their usefulness to society, they forgot what was essential and universal in Jewish and non-Jewish history. One day, without much preparation, I sat down and began to write my first book, *Satan in Goray*.

While I wrote it, I had the feeling that I was entranced, and that an unseen being was dictating to me. I didn't need to do much research, because my childhood and my entire past has prepared me for this little volume. Also, I was myself steeped in all the neuroses which I described. There was a sort of divine hysteria in our family. All of us were possessed by dybbuks. People often ask me if I read Freud before I wrote *Satan in Goray*. I barely knew the name. I could truthfully say that all the complexes of Freud, Jung, and Adler were in me. The most wild and heretic ideas ran through my mind.[1] There was a sensuality in me that frightened me. I had dreams which made me believe that I was on the verge of insanity. My nights were full of demons and hobgoblins rummaging among the books in my father's library.

When this book came out in Warsaw, the critics in America attacked me, complaining that it was not written in the Yiddish tradition. They contended that what I wrote about the Jews was food for antisemites. However, there were a few who defended me. These people were as violently for me as the others were opposed to my novel. Thank God, I was controversial from the very beginning, and I hope to remain that way to the end. It is not the obligation of any writer to write according to a tradition, a literary school, an accepted style. Writers must bring their own goals and methods to their work. I must admit that even my brother, I. J. Singer, was somehow bewildered by what his junior had done. It was not so much the content of what I wrote as my light-minded independence of the opinions of others. He said to me jokingly that the Yiddishists would never forgive me and that I was committing literary suicide.

My brother himself was in the process of writing his novel *The Brothers Ashkenazi*, where he described with great skill both the social conditions of an epoch and the fate of unique characters. My brother was deeply interested in social problems and social values. He still believed that humanity might learn from its mistakes and correct them. We had many discussions on this

topic, I taking the part of the extreme pessimist. He knew everything I knew, but I certainly did not know what he had experienced both in Poland before I grew up and in Russia in the time
of the revolution. Toward the end of his life, in the time of the
Hitler destruction, he was inclined to admit that humanity
seemed hopeless. But he pointed out that there were millions
and millions of good people whose only shortcoming was their
passivity. The Hitlers and their like always rely on the submis-
siveness and long-term suffering of those who reject violence
under all conditions. I would never have reached even the little
I reached without my brother's help—his criticism and encouragement. Destiny had it that we were given separate fields of
literary endeavor so that there was never the slightest feeling of
competition between us.

I have never yet dedicated this book to anybody, but I dedicate
it to him now with a feeling of admiration and reverence. He was
not only my beloved brother, but my literary father and master.
While writing this book I remembered the most important rule
he gave me for writing fiction: to let the events speak for themselves and never to intrude with interpretation. It is a great satisfaction for me that my brother's works are being published again
both in the United States and in many other countries—and that
he is getting some of the recognition he deserved. To me he was
one of the most important writers of this century.

To the True Protester

Wolf and sheep in carnal embrace,
What God will ever show them his face?
God Himself, the Lord of Creation
Has decreed upon them bloodshed, privation[1]
There is one redeemer of God's cruel game
The only Messiah—Death is his name
He's wolf's and sheep's only grace
Men's everlasting resting place
Beaten protester, wary of life
Don't build a house, don't take a wife
Don't bring up children to suffer the fate
Of God's injustice, man's lies and hate.[2]
Yesterday's victim is the oppressor today
There is no hope, there is no way,
In our protest do we cry
Why doest Thou punish the helpless, why?
Thine is the wisdom and the might
While we are blind in the darkest night.

This poem, handwritten in the original English, is undated, though it appears on the back of a letter sent by the Carl Hanser Verlag, dated August 13, 1980. It foregrounds the philosophy of protest which Singer discusses in his author's note to *The Penitent* (1983) and in his memoir, *Love and Exile* (1984), while also providing a subtle yet counterbalancing voice of faith in the divine, and in acceptance of the limits of being human.

Singer the Editor

AN AFTERWORD ON THE EDITORIAL PROCESS

Isaac Bashevis Singer's essays show that his artistry was grounded in a clearly articulated theoretical framework. Yet this articulation itself elides an aspect of Singer's literary practice: his meticulous work as translator and editor. Apart from organizing and introducing Singer's essays, collecting his work has also involved an intimate and thorough investigation of his complex creative process, which generally began in Yiddish, written by hand into small notebooks or on loose-leaf paper. These handwritten manuscripts were often sent directly to the *Forverts* for typesetting and printing without any intermediary stage. Later, Singer would cut out clippings for translation—itself a long process that involved sitting with a collaborator who served mostly as a stenographer, typing as Singer orally translated himself, word by word, directly from the printed Yiddish text. These draft translations were given to Singer, who worked over them himself directly in English, with sentences rewritten, sections cut, and additions made in longhand. The corrected versions were then typed up again by collaborators into clean drafts that were edited by Singer yet again, with additional corrections, repeating the process until he had a final draft. Once this draft was ready, it would either be read aloud as a lecture, or sent out for publication—at which point Singer would go through another revision with an editor, and see the text again in the final proofs, where he often undertook additional fine-tuning. This process led Singer to call the published English versions of his work "second originals."*

Any effort to publish Singer's essays must also take into account this complex creative process. For example, the Yiddish original of "Who Needs Literature?" first appeared in late 1963, every other week, under three discrete titles, in the Sunday edition of the *Forverts*, all with the name Yitskhok Varshavski in the byline.[†] What seemed to be separate articles, each of which consisted of about 2,000 words, was in reality a single long-form essay on the nature of the literary arts, which would have benefited from being published as a whole in a Yiddish literary journal. But it never appeared as a standalone essay in Yiddish. Rather, the sections were translated into English and, after being brought back together, edited down to such an extent that the work was completely transformed. The English version is less than 3,500 words, nearly half the length of the original Yiddish essay. The kinds of revisions that Singer made can be seen on the article's first page, which has been reworked to such an extent, and with so much added in

---

* This much-quoted phrase was used by Singer in a 1969 interview with Cyrena Pondrom (*Conversations* 1992, 49), and was developed in his author's note to *A Friend of Kafka and Other Stories* (1970), where he writes: "I have translated these stories with the assistance of collaborators, and I find that I do much revision in the process of translation. It is not an exaggeration to say that over the years English has become my 'second' language."

[†] Singer, "Tsu vos literatur?" (Who Needs Literature?, Oct. 20, 1963), "Keyn shum shrayber shraybt nit 'far'n shufald'" (No Writer Writes "For the Drawer," Nov. 3, 1963), and "Vos iz di tsukunft fun dem kinstlerlishn vort?" (What Is the Future of the Artistic Word?, Nov. 17, 1963).

1

There are times when I wonder what purpose ~~fictional~~ ~~literature~~ serves today. Why fabricate plots when nature ~~and~~ ~~human~~ life unfold$ an inexhaustible wealth of ~~happenings~~ *events* , more strange than anything ~~fiction~~ *Literature* might offer? Fantasy will never be able to match all the surprising twists that fact is made of. No pen has been able to produce a work so true and free of imperfections as ~~is any story based on fact, such as we may read~~ *or The proceedings* ~~in~~ a case history ~~or how~~ in a courtroom. Just as there is no ~~such thing as~~ a perfect crime, so ~~too~~ there *is no* ~~never can be a~~ perfect novel. Even <u>Anna Karenina</u> and <u>Madame Bovary</u> reveal ~~flaws and inconsistencies that are part of all fiction.~~

Sometimes I am afraid that, sooner or later, men will arrive at the conclusion that reading fiction is a waste of time.

But why should this thought frighten me? Is it just because I would be one of the victims?

It's not just this. Fiction represents a highly intellectual challenge. Even if a ~~machine~~ *machine or computer* could be invented ~~that would be~~ capable of relating to us ~~in detail~~ *what great new modern* the experiences of a ~~Raskolnikov~~, of a ~~Madame Bovary~~ or an ~~Anna Karenina~~ *American*, it would still be interesting to find out ~~whether the same end~~ *what happened to our imagination and it's Instrument the language. Why did* ~~could not be achieved by way of the pen.~~ *As a matter of fact Expression* ~~That literature is still produced by the old methods is due solely to the fact that there is no such machine as yet--~~

It would be a lot more difficult for us to make peace with a literary machine than with a counting and computing machine. If a machine could tell ~~That literature is still produced by the old method is due to the fact that there is no such machine as yet--~~

English, that it is difficult in parts to make out the original material.

Given the extent of Singer's editorial work, an inherent dilemma arises with any effort to collect his essays: whether or not, in drafts for which no final version exists or in final versions found with earlier drafts, to include excised portions on the grounds that they offer insight into his creative process and the fuller extent of his thought.

This concern is clearly visible in "A Personal Concept of Religion." Like other works, the Yiddish original first appeared in the *Forverts* as three discrete pieces with three separate titles, under the pseudonymous byline Yitskhok Varshavski—not in the special Sunday edition, like his works on literature, but on weekdays, on random pages, without any attention given to their intellectual value.*

The marked-up draft of this essay shows how Singer distilled his ideas as part of the translation and editing process. This can be seen in the following example, where took a paragraph translated from the Yiddish original and cut out the middle—where his logic is developed and the ideas are spelled out in detail—leaving only the beginning and end of his conceptual trajectory:

> If religion must be closely bound with revelation, then I cannot properly call myself a religious person. It is true that I believe in God and even in his ability to reveal himself. But I cannot base my belief on actual revelation. Personally,

---

* Singer, "A perzenlikhe oyffasung fun religie" (A Personal Conception of Religion, Aug. 9, 1966), "Di getlikhe kunst un dos getlikhe visn" (Divine Art and Divine Knowledge, Aug. 10, 1966), and "Mayn bagrif vegn got un di flikhtn fun mentsh" (My Concept of God and the Duties of Man, Aug. 11, 1966).

~~I have never experienced one. Those that are described in holy books have not convinced me of their authenticity.~~ But, at the same time, I believe—without revelation—that there is a God who rules the world and keeps watch over us. I often pray to this God although I have no clear conception of what he is, what his demands are, nor what his aims and motives are.

Upon rereading his raw material, now translated into English, Singer appears to decide that the intricacies of his personal opinion are less important than the general premise and final conclusion—and that he does not, ultimately, need the middle part of this paragraph. In this way, he also omits part of his thought process while emphasizing his broader ideas. In some cases, he deletes an entire paragraph in order to maintain conceptual continuity:

> God does reveal himself, but gradually—line by line. He demands the reader's trust, but if the reader refuses to trust him and becomes impatient, he cannot help him.

> ~~Like every artist, God is sensitive. Perhaps He wasn't too happy when Spinoza described him as some sort of lifeless machine. He probably was hurt by the twaddle of Feuerbach; however, he may also be vexed by those who profess to speak in his name and who pretend to be privy to all his secrets. The praise is often as petty as the blasphemy. A Creator must possess much patience.~~

> The greatest misunderstanding rampant among God's readers is in their concept of death. Nearly all of them are convinced that when a chapter ends, so does the novel. But to allow the readers to remember all the chapters is impossible. . . .

-2-

~~ability to reveal Himself. But I cannot base my belief~~
~~on actual revelation. Personally, I have never experi-~~
~~enced one. Those that are described in holy books have~~
~~not convinced me of their authenticity.~~

But at the same time, I believe -- without
revelation -- that there is a God who rules the world
and keeps watch over it. I often pray to this God, ~~who~~ *although*
~~perhaps has never revealed Himself to anyone,~~
I have no clear conception of what He is, what His demands are, nor what His aims and motives are.

I have made peace with the concept that it is
possible -- at least for me -- to serve a God who is
silent. At the same time, my God is ~~neither~~ *not* Spinoza's
~~nor an~~ indifferent Nature, but a God with all the divine
attributes. ~~Although I studied Spinoza's "Ethics" for~~
~~years, I never was convinced that~~ God lacks will, purpose or compassion, ~~and that~~ For Him there is no good
or evil. ~~It is true that I lack positive proof that~~
He ~~does have~~ *has no* will, purpose ~~and a~~ sense of justice. ~~It~~
~~was proven a long time ago that man's mind is too lim-~~
~~ited to solve this problem,~~ *answer question* ~~just as it cannot square a~~
~~circle, or build a perpetual motion machine.~~ But I have
built for myself a private God; ~~you might even label~~
~~him an idol.~~ I've endowed my God with all the properties
and attributes that appeal to me. I've fashioned Him

FIGURE 3. From a draft of Singer's essay "A Personal Concept of Religion," with his handwritten edits and corrections in English. Isaac Bashevis Singer Papers, Harry Ransom Center, University of Texas at Austin.

The cut paragraph is not in itself uninteresting, but it seems to take the essay into ideas that distract from its main message—which focuses on the connection between literature and faith and a portrayal of the godhead as a creative artist. In mentioning Spinoza and Feuerbach, he risks losing his audience and undermining the ideas that drive the essay in the first place. Translation practice, editorial concerns, and consideration of his audience all influence the final formulations of his essay.

The dilemma of Singer's revisions gives rise to a basic question: how much access to provide into Singer's creative process? If the essays appear in their final versions alone, Singer's edits are passed directly into the published version, and the current volume adds little beyond collecting and organizing the work. If the essays are published with all excised sections reinstated, Singer's choices are betrayed in a way that directly contradicts markings indicating his intentions. For these reasons, and many more beyond enumeration, I decided on a middle ground, marking excised sections consisting of full phrases with Arabic numerals and reproducing them as endnotes at the back of the book.

There remain two main issues to mention regarding the editorial process.

The first has to do with linguistic conventions common in Singer's time, or inherited from past decades, that have since received more scrutiny—more in the English language than in Yiddish. At the center of these conventions is the use of gendered pronouns to represent general categories—the artist, the writer, the reader—to which the text often refers in the masculine. As always, considering the importance of readability to Singer's work, and the understanding that he was not necessarily invested in the idea of the artist as a man alone—and, especially, in light of his repeated treatment of gender issues in his fiction—I decided to shift the language whenever it did not change the meaning of the text.* The Yiddish word *mentsh*, for example, which usually translates literally as "man" and is often used this way to denote the general idea of an individual, has been here rendered as "person," especially as Singer deploys this same choice in his translation of "A Personal Concept of Religion," in which the word *mentsh* appears specifically as *person*. As for the issue of general categories, these have been, whenever possible, moved into the plural—appearing as writers, artists, and readers—to make them gender-neutral. The only case in which this step would have involved more intervention than might have been appropriate is the case of God. Singer's thinking on divinity was complex enough, I believe, to think of God as something far beyond a person. Yet—except when he specifically spoke of God's feminine aspects from a kabbalistic perspective—his references to God were, in the tradition of his time's discourse, made with the masculine pronoun. Were Singer alive today to be consulted on the matter, I believe he might have considered using gender-neutral language for God. But he is not alive, and so all references to God remain as they appeared in the original.

All other issues, such as spelling variations between Cabala and Kabbalah, have been updated to the most common current usage. Such changes are minor, but they have major implications for readability and relevance to our times. Ultimately, anyone interested in Singer's original manuscripts can always refer to them at the Harry Ransom Center in Austin, Texas.

The last editorial challenge concerns essays for which no Yiddish original could be found. This includes two important essays: "The Kabbalah and Modern Times" and "Why I Write

* For discussions of gender in Singer's work, see Warren Hoffman (2009) and Jill Salberg (2012).

As I Do: The Philosophy and Definition of a Jewish Writer."
Both works present core elements of Singer's development as a
writer and thinker. In the case of the first, though no entry
matching this title or topic appears in any existing bibliography,
in an article published under the name Yitskhok Varshavski on
March 2, 1965, Singer does mention giving a lecture with this
title at the University of Michigan and Wayne College.* There
is also an audio recording of the lecture given at the 1976 Panarion Conference.† As for the second essay, several typescript
drafts exist in English, with Singer's handwritten corrections,
including a version that is marked as copied on March 21, 1967,
from an original dated April 10, 1962. Again, no entry in any
existing bibliography matches this essay, but Singer did return
to it, using it as an introduction to *Gifts*, a limited-edition collection of five stories published in 1985 by the Jewish Publication Society, which included the title story, "Matones," published in Yiddish. In these cases and others, the known dates are
given, with the understanding that the original Yiddish text
might have been written months, years, or decades earlier.

Singer did not begin to regularly translate and publish his
work in English until the early 1960s. At that point, he had
nearly four decades of material already written and waiting to
be translated—and he was also constantly producing new
work. His story collections were never produced synchronic-
ally: stories that appeared in a single collection could have been
written decades apart and were organized thematically, or with
a particular rhythm between stories—for example, between
those set in the past and those set in the present, or stories of

---

* Singer, "Yidish in di amerikaner univerzitetn" (Yiddish in American Universities, *Forverts*, March 2, 1965).

† Singer papers, Harry Ransom Center.

personal tragedy and stories of supernatural miracles, stories told by a Singer-like narrator and stories told by an old-world gossip who often bore the name of his own aunt, Yentl. As such, taking into account his close collaboration with editors who prepared his work for publication, I have adopted a multi-pronged approach in arranging the pieces in this collection: on the one hand, I have separated the essays into three broad categories, offering a view onto the central themes in Singer's work, and, on the other, within each category, I have put the essays in chronological order, providing a view onto the development of his thinking. In cases when the Yiddish or English publication history of an essay is unknown, or cannot be estimated, the essay has been placed at the section's end.

The essays that are included in this collection are, ultimately, those that proved to offer a clear and representative range of the themes and ideas that Singer wrote about in his work. Yet I should note what this collection does *not* include. First, aside from works of fiction and memoir that were translated in Singer's lifetime but have yet to be published, this collection leaves out his literary criticism—including articles about writers as diverse as Franz Kafka, Bruno Schulz, Knut Hamsun, Sholem Aleichem, I. L. Peretz, Conrad Richter, Barton Midwood, Frederic Prokosch, Aaron Zeitlin, and his brother I. J. Singer. The reason is simple: these works, while interesting as reflections on certain authors, represent a small portion of the reviews that Singer wrote in Yiddish, and lack the focus of his essays. Including them would offer readers only a partial picture of Singer as a literary critic, and would also detract from the integrity of the collection as a whole. Second, no work was newly translated for the collection, simply because, as mentioned, the pieces translated by Singer represent the author's implicit selection. In addition, since Singer often returned to the same material, repurposing portions in new essays on related themes, I have omitted those essays that repeated ideas he develops in greater detail elsewhere. Those that were published in his lifetime have been included in a separate list appearing at the end of the bibliography. Finally, several acceptance speeches found in the archives, while interesting in their own right, were ultimately beyond the scope of this collection.

Working with Singer's unpublished material for nearly a decade, I can testify to the fact that the job is never done. Discoveries keep being made, new information is continually revealed, and additional facets of his literary and intellectual pursuits keep coming to light. This collection, which consolidates several decades of critical thinking, is only a first step toward fostering a deeper understanding of Singer's literary achievement and inviting further reconsiderations of his artistic legacy.

ACKNOWLEDGMENTS

Every book project has its obstacles and triumphs—and this volume is no exception. Its inception was rooted in a nagging curiosity about the theoretical framework on which Isaac Bashevis Singer built his deceptively simple art. Satisfying this curiosity took me on a decade-long adventure across continents, during which I met many people who helped to make this book a reality.

At the Hebrew University of Jerusalem, I was supported by Professors Leona Toker, Eli Lederhendler, Avraham Novershtern, Shira Wolosky, Uzi Rebhun, and Menahem Blondheim. They made it possible for me to follow any and all leads on this literary adventure. I developed the project while a doctoral student in the Department of English, and later continued as a postdoctoral fellow supported by the Golda Meir Fellowship Trust, the Institute for Contemporary Jewry, the program in Yiddish, and the Daat Hamakom research group.

At the Harry Ransom Center, University of Texas at Austin, I was supported by the Edwin Gale Fellowship and the Dorot Foundation Postdoctoral Research Fellowship in Jewish Studies, and warmly welcomed by Professor Robert Abzug. I would like to thank the entire staff at the Ransom Center for their help, and especially Elizabeth Garver for her efforts during my first trip to the HRC in 2014 and my subsequent trips in 2016 and 2017, and for digitally filling my last-minute queries during the lockdown months of the coronavirus pandemic in 2020 and 2021. Thanks are due as well to my good friend Andi Gustavson, who helped me navigate Austin during my time in the city.

I spent considerable time on this project working at the New York Public Library in a variety of capacities. I was a Short-Term Fellow in 2015, undertaking research in the Dorot Jewish Division, and I would like to thank Stephen D. Corrsin and Amanda (Miryem-Khaye) Seigel for their help during that time. Throughout that year, I was also a scholar in the Center for Research in the Humanities, working in the Wertheim Room, and spent time in the Astor Reading Room for Rare Books and Manuscripts. I was also a Fordham/NYPL Short-Term Research Fellow in Jewish Studies in 2018, and am grateful to Carolyn Broomhead and Professor Magda Teter for their efforts in organizing that visit. I am indebted to the entire staff in all of the NYPL's divisions, in particular Melanie Locay, who helped me keep my bearings as I traveled back and forth between New York and Jerusalem, and Rebecca Federman, who, during the coronavirus pandemic, was able to help with digital duplication of essays and articles which I otherwise would not have been able to access.

I also worked on this project at the Center for Jewish History's Lillian Goldman Reading Room—part of it as a Vladimir and Pearl Heifetz Memorial Fellow and Vivian Lefsky Hort Memorial Fellow in East European Jewish Literature of the YIVO Institute for Jewish Research. For their support and guidance during my time at the CJH, I would like to thank Eddy Portnoy and the staff in both the general reading room and the YIVO offices. During this period, I received a Research Fellowship from the Memorial Foundation for Jewish Culture, and want to extend my gratitude for their support as well.

While conducting research on Singer's essays, I also delved deeply into his life and work, and this understanding contributed to my efforts to collect and edit this volume. This activity, which was not always directly connected with the essays, involved close cooperation with individuals across the literary landscape, creating the broader context for this work. I would like to thank Deborah Treisman, fiction editor at *The New Yorker*, whose interest in Singer's stories helped ignite my direct engagement with his writing. Several other editors, many of them scholars, also published either edited versions of these essays, or else new translations of thematically related work, among them Saul Noam Zarrit, Val Vinokur, Boris Dralyuk, Kelly Burdick, and Madeleine Cohen—all of whom I wish to thank for their interest and attention. Sometimes, in addition to professional cooperation, we also need moral support, and for this I would like to thank Professors David Roskies and Ofer Dynes. I am especially indebted to poet and translator Peter Cole, without whom this project might still be an idea rather than a reality, and both to him and to Adina Hoffman for catching everything I missed along the way. I am also grateful to the entire team at Princeton University Press, in particular Anne Savarese, who shepherded the project, Jodi Beder, who made the final version as consistent and readable as possible, and Ellen Foos, whose experience and flexibility helped make this a better book.

I want to express my deep gratitude to the team that coalesced in parallel to this project—which began with my meeting Singer's son, Israel Zamir, a year before his passing, and continued with my acquaintance with Zamir's children, Singer's grandchildren, who today make up the Isaac Bashevis Singer Literary Trust. Their faith in my efforts has allowed us to continue Singer's work where it was left off when he passed away in 1991. And we all owe an expression of gratitude to Susan Schulman and the staff of the Susan Schulman Literary Agency, where Singer's writing is championed on a daily basis.

Finally, I would like to acknowledge my own family—Aleza, little Kedem Sarai, and even littler Alma Zisel—who fill me with the kind of strength that no theoretical framework can ever provide.

NOTES

Who Needs Literature?

1. *The next paragraph begins with this crossed-out sentence:* That literature is still produced by the old methods is due solely to the fact that there is no such machine as yet—thank goodness.

2. *Crossed out:* In a great and wealthy nation such as ours, works of poetry frequently come out in editions of five hundred copies, and even of these many are distributed by the authors among their friends.

3. *Crossed out:* It doesn't take much skill to win sensational victories in chess when one of the partners can start out with writers who, desiring to act the part of revolutionaries, attempt to create new literary rules without real knowledge of the original rules. Their argument is that human intellect must not be made to conform to cut-and-dried principles. My answer to their contentions is that a revolution that consists of devising new names for existing things is not a renaissance. If you want to call soda water champagne, you won't change anything. We may dress up doormen to look like admirals, but that won't make any difference in the armed forces.

4. *The next paragraph is crossed out:* Parasites grow and develop best on a sick body. Instead of blaming the parasites, we would do better to examine the host body to find out why it should be unable to fend off the hanger-on.

5. *Crossed out:* Many readers studied literature in order to acquire the rudiments of grammar—to learn how to construct a sentence.

6. *Crossed out:* from the radio, the movies, the press, and television.

7. *Crossed out:* to have an important place in modern life

8. *Crossed out:* which are now discussed in detail in college classes, on the radio, and frequently from the pulpits of churches and synagogues.

9. *Crossed out:* A manuscript gathering dust in a desk drawer never brought recognition.

10. *The next paragraph begins with this crossed-out sentence:* The secret of prose writing has always been the ability to tell a story in such a manner as to arouse the reader's interest and to reveal human individuality.

11. *The next paragraph is crossed out:* Every true work of art, no matter how narrowly defined or specific in character, is surrounded by an aura of eternity. Every work of art represents both a protest and a prayer to God.

12. *The next paragraph is crossed out:* The forces with which the creative artist will have to contend in the future will be such that only the most ethical of creative artists will have a chance to survive. In the final analysis, the aesthetic and the ethical elements will meet and become one. They always do.

Old Truths and New Clichés

1. *Crossed out:* They did not become involved in any outside observations. They sat, by themselves, in their rooms and wrote about lands they had never visited and about peoples they never knew.

2. *Crossed out:* and had long since lost its biological function.

3. *Crossed out:* Research has become a business for industry and government.

4. *Crossed out:* in human nature.

5. *Crossed out:* Yes, science is, again, in danger of inheriting a new Aristotle, who will, with his authority, direct and halt altogether the way ahead of science. It is a fact that half the world bases its sociology and even its art on one authority—Karl Marx or Lenin. In the democratic half of the world, art becomes more intellectual, symbolic, psychological, and often even Leninistic. Interpretation becomes more important than observation. A number of writers are not satisfied with merely describing and storytelling. They interpret their own observations. Readers become more and more dependent on guides without knowing how to read and understand art themselves. Now, one can never get a guide telling one how to read such clear authors as Chekhov, Maupassant, and Dickens.

6. *Crossed out:* all the more like a riddle one must solve, like a dream that one must interpret.

7. *Crossed out:* Many modernists perform the tricks that young boys have been performing for years: they paint mustaches over women's lips. The trouble with such tricks is that they soon lose the little humor they possessed in the first place. Many painters now do the same as Chagall—they place their figures upside down. A great number try to copy Picasso's spitefulness. Originality becomes banality.

8. *Crossed out:* The number of poets who have ceased to use punctuation now reaches into the thousands. From something that should be an act of high originality, it has become an empty foolish cliché, a fashion. I believe the same will happen with buildings that look like screwdrivers.

9. *Crossed out:* looking inward, studying their own souls

10. *Crossed out:* Tolstoy and Dostoevsky had more insight into themselves than Kafka and Joyce. Cezanne and Manet had more originality than Chagall and Picasso.

Gogol and Turgenev described Russian society, its economy and politics, better than have the Soviet Leninists.

11. *Crossed out:* distorted. The same proves true when art is hypnotized by authority or a small number of authorities.

12. *Crossed out:* boredom, and self-analysis, which psychoanalysts listen to only because they are being paid to do so. Most of these confessions are boring and lacking in originality.

13. *Crossed out:* There could have existed only one Raskolnikov even if Dostoevsky had concerned himself with criminology. We have, here, an example of how external observation and contemplation are so connected that it is impossible to know where one ends and the other begins.

14. *Crossed out:* of all censorship

15. *Crossed out:* its description

16. *Original sentence:* Those who use it most often use foul language instead of giving the reader the combination of sex and character, which is necessary for good literature.

17. *Crossed out:* and do not reveal anything to them that they did not already know.

18. *Crossed out:* attempt to shock readers as if they were children who were just discovering the facts of life from their novels.

19. *Crossed out:* suspense and

20. *Crossed out:* and needed this information from these writers.

21. *Crossed out:* This is the concern of the political journal, the brochure, and the professional movement.

22. *Crossed out:* It is like the waves of the sea that have great force but cannot be harnessed to create energy, because they do not flow in one direction.

23. *Crossed out:* as the devil does incense.

24. *Crossed out:* This is true even of so great a writer as Thomas Mann. His *Magic Mountain* is loosely constructed.

25. *Crossed out:* essays or even merely fragments.

26. *Crossed out:* as Aldous Huxley does in his novel *Point Counter Point,* in which every word and gesture of his characters is explained and psychoanalyzed.

27. *Crossed out:* writers who set themselves against society.

28. *Crossed out:* The greatest masters of all times were not angry and made no serious efforts to reform society or to destroy it. In their early years, a few, like Dostoevsky, took up with revolutionary ideas, but often, in their ripe years, they discarded them.

29. *Crossed out:* people cannot radically alter history or their fates, and that

30. *Crossed out:* and, in a sense, provincial

31. *Crossed out:* One cannot compare El Greco with Raphael.

32. *The following paragraph is crossed out:* When Shakespeare said, "The play is the thing," he meant the story above all. In our times, storytelling is becoming a lost art. Their art requires supposed originality and interpretation.

33. *Crossed out (slashes represent line breaks):* and hysteria. / Modern artists are so fearful of being old-fashioned and conservative that they have discarded lasting truths and replaced them with polished clichés. / The great art industry attempts to deny beauty and inborn talent, which it tramples with strong rebellion and with an art that is crooked, lame, disharmonious, and crippled. Impotence calls itself potency and a thousand impotents cry—*Amen.*

34. *This long section, ultimately crossed out after repeated revisions, incorporates cuts from two separate edits in English, the latter of which cuts out an entire page and a half of this essay (brackets represent earlier cuts, slashes represent line breaks):* It is untrue that one can teach talentless people to write, to paint, or even to act. Talent comes with genetics, and only later ripens with the environment. Talents are born, though they must learn and develop themselves. / [From the day we are born we carry our excellent points and our strengths within us.] One cannot teach anyone to be a Dostoevsky or a Van Gogh. Moreover, neither Dostoevsky nor Van Gogh could have explained themselves or analyzed how they created or why. Analysis belongs not to the artist, but to the critic. The truth is that artists seldom understand what critics write about them, or what their aims are. Modern critics with their search in every creation for social elements can have that which is needed for literary science, but artists, their methods and instincts, are not touched. The thousands of volumes written about Shakespeare have all failed to explain what Shakespeare was and why his works have endured. In general, art is not something for explanation or interpretation. When Gertrude Stein said that a rose is a rose is a rose, she meant that a rose speaks for itself, and that a thousand words about a rose could not explain the wonder and pleasure that a rose gives us. I am not against literary criticism and interpretation. However, one cannot analyze a rose, a sunset, or a soap bubble. And it would have been a great tragedy if the rose, itself, would have taken to analyzing its colors, or if the sunset would have thought over what kind of dust it needed to create its colors. This is just what Nabokov and others like him are doing, although they are far, far from roses. / In our age of progress, revolution, rebellion, analysis, fabricated originality, and pseudo-psychology, it is dangerous to make people recall old and eternal truths. This has the flavor of reaction and even, perhaps, counterrevolution. But I dare to say that without any old truths, art cannot exist. Artists cannot ignore outward nature and concentrate on self-analysis. They are not analysts or commentators. They are not, by nature, rebels or social reformers. Forced originality is not the same as uniqueness and individuality. Artists are not teachers, but entertainers, creators. They are not capable of waging wars. They cannot be leaders in the struggle between

peoples or classes. They have a strong feeling for justice, but they are not prophets, although many critics have crowned their favorite writers with this title. / Many modern literary critics have, among other things, forgotten the difference between entertaining the public and exciting it. One has the concept so confused that what emerges is—everything exciting is art. It is true that art has an element of shock. We become very disturbed by a work of art, but not all that disturbs us is art. There are, in our day, hundreds of books commemorating the Hitler holocaust which disturb the reader to the very marrow of his bones, but they are not art. Especially in America, the expression "excitement" is a synonym for art. This word is misguiding in literature, in cinema, in theater, and even in music. One does not need talent to shake nerves. The newspapers do this daily. / Yes, running away from the old innocent clichés, many modern writers are falling into new and dangerous clichés which do enormous damage to the art of our time. / If the novel, the painting, the sculpture, or the theater do not want to have the same end as modern poetry, [i.e. the loss of the consumer, influence, and metamorphosis into a production for those with dubious fine taste] . . . Still, artists of our generation must return to a number of concepts that they have eliminated as outdated. / Creative people must, before everything else, free themselves from the megalomaniacal idea that they are and must be the spiritual leaders of their generation—teachers, leaders, or prophets. The artist is never more than an entertainer. Great artists have entertained the intellectual and sensitive people of their generation. This is completely sufficient. Art is, at no time, to go farther than this. What was appropriate for Homer and Shakespeare is appropriate for our time. / There can be no ugly art. Works that have no beauty are not art. People cannot define just what beauty is, but many possess an instinct for it, exactly as they do for color and tone.

35. *Crossed out:* I have seen many uneducated people excited by Van Gogh's pictures, with Michelangelo's *Moses*, with the plays of Molière and Strindberg, with the novels of Tolstoy, Dostoevsky, and Gogol, with such epics is *Eugene Onegin* and *Pan Tadeusz*, and with such buildings as St. Peter's Cathedral and Notre Dame.

36. *Crossed out:* and that his whole epoch is wild.

37. *Crossed out:* like talent itself, comes from the genes

38. *Crossed out:* No true artist sets out to look for originality. On the contrary,

39. *Crossed out:* Banality, like originality, cannot be overcome. / Art cannot and must not compete with science, history, or the infinite facts connected with various other disciplines. Life has always been richer than fiction. An actual sunset is richer in colors than the best painting. A news item in a newspaper sometimes contains more spiritual dynamite than the most powerful novel. Confessions by criminals and psychopaths often exceed all idiosyncrasies that art can convey. The goal of art is not to stimulate people, but to give a kind of satisfaction that only talent can offer. If perhaps it would have been possible to solve the riddle of art, the solution would lie

in biology, not sociology. The same powers that work in artists produce plants from the earth, and develop the embryo in the mother's womb.

40. *Crossed out:* Conditions change only on the surface, not in essence.

41. *Crossed out:* They can imitate the geniuses, but at no time use their achievements.

42. *Crossed out:* solipsistic

43. *Crossed out:* it is synthetic, built on experience and contact with people and nature.

44. *Crossed out:* Entertainers cannot create from themselves alone.

45. *Crossed out:* create and lead

46. *Crossed out:* In this sense, every artist is mystical.

Literature for Children and Adults

1. *Crossed out:* He might have also conceded that the language expressing these emotions or affects could not convey all their potential combinations.

2. *Crossed out:* No cry, no laughter, no shouts or gestures can convey to us how someone is feeling. Deeds can only communicate results and desires, not the inner processes.

3. *Crossed out:* consciously broke the literary rules.

4. *Crossed out:* It yearns to overwhelm the jaded reviewer, the hack seeking a theme, the film producer coveting a sensation.

5. *Crossed out:* as is the case among many of those who speak in the name of a false liberalism.

6. *Crossed out:* There has evolved a method of child-rearing intended to offer an alternative to the Ten Commandments.

7. *Crossed out:* and—as a matter of course—for all authority.

8. *Crossed out:* of his convictions

9. *Crossed out:* to destroy civilization and

10. *Crossed out:* I often have the feeling that America is in danger of slipping into this kind of cultural suicide.

11. *Crossed out:* of good deeds and sins.

12. *Crossed out:* no true act

13. *Crossed out:* love of beauty

The Spirit of Judaism

1. *In a later version, published as an introduction to Ira Moskowitz's book* The Hasidim (1973), *the opening sentence reads:* As I'm writing this I see before me pictures of religious Jews in the Williamsburg section of Brooklyn, as well as a number of

sketches and lithographs of Hasidic Jews in Israel prepared by my friend Ira Moskowitz.

Yiddish, the Language of Exile

1. *This is a translation of* U'mipnei hata'einu galinu mei'artzeinu—*from the* musaf *liturgy recited on festivals.*

2. *The following paragraph is crossed out:* Among those who looked upon the exile as something positive were the Assimilationists, who were a product of the Emancipation, as well as the Bundists and communists, for whom the yearning for Israel was nothing more than a religious dream, a Messianic fantasy that could never be realized. The slogan of these leftist Jews was to fight wherever we are for a "better world," one in which there would be no Jews nor Gentiles, but a united humanity whose only goal would be progress in every field.

3. *Crossed out:* Jewishness was our very existence.

4. *Crossed out:* for the Jews to return to

5. *Crossed out:* in the promised land

6. *Crossed out:* in its spiritual progression

7. *Crossed out:* Moses, who killed an Egyptian and later married an Ethiopian woman

8. *The earlier version reads:* The Holy Constantine could never make peace with the idea that the Song of Songs was nothing more than a grand love poem, and that King David enticed women away from their husbands.

9. *The earlier version reads:* The secular, Hebrew writer pronounced worldliness and progress in a language which was unworldly and tightly bound with what they called the "mold of generations."

10. *The earlier version reads:* and it was foreseen that the *shtetls* would be replaced by the Kolkhoz, the complex of Zavods or factories, and by the agents of world revolution.

11. *The earlier version reads:* The Hitler Holocaust destroyed the greatest part of Yiddish-speaking Jews west of the Iron Curtain.

12. *The earlier version reads:* To me, the certainty of the enlightened ones that the world is a result of chemical or physical accident is nothing more than a revised version of the ancient idolatry. As a Jewish writer, I am shocked at the form that modern art has taken. Paintings and sculptures are becoming utterly abstract, without an "address," rootless, and arbitrary. Literature is turning totally vulgar, pornographic, and insipid. The modern Jew's only ambition is "to be like all nations" and the nations themselves are becoming a hodgepodge of cultures, a generation like that which built the Tower of Babel. Life abounds in more luxuries, but loses the very juices which sustain its vitality. It is a pseudo-affluence, the essence of which is sheer boredom.

13. *The earlier version reads:* Empires fall, but cultures thrive.

14. *In the earlier version, Stalin is missing and instead Singer writes "Nassers," referring to former Egyptian president Gamal Abdel Nasser (1918–1970).*

15. *In the earlier version, "national rebirth" appears as "physical resurrection."*

16. *The earlier version reads:* They were and remain watchers in the night. Their culture in Hebrew, Aramaic, and Yiddish will inspire the cultural growth of all people.

Yiddish Theater Lives, Despite the Past

1. *The following paragraph does not appear in* The New York Times *article, only in the typescript in the Singer papers.*

2. *Crossed out:* They have all the suspense and much more than the theater of cynicism and materialism could ever attain.

Yiddish and Jewishness

1. *The earlier draft reads:* There are Jews in whom Jewishness approaches the vanishing point and others in whom it assumes a great magnitude. But no Jews can escape their heritage entirely.

2. *The earlier draft reads:* to destroy itself

3. *The earlier draft reads:* As I have already pointed out, the Enlightenment gave birth to contradictory tendencies, on the one hand a movement toward total assimilation, and on the other a resurgence of Jewish nationalism.

4. *Crossed out:* and although of course his effort failed

5. *Crossed out:* to show human life in all circumstances

Why I Write As I Do

1. *The lecture draft begins this way:* When I was invited to speak before this distinguished audience, I knew in advance.

2. *This story eventually appeared in Singer's last English-language collection* The Death of Methuselah and Other Stories *(1988).*

3. *The following paragraph, which is not crossed out in the latest draft in the Singer papers, is missing from both the 1974 and 1985 versions of the essay:* Since everything issued from potentiality, there could be no difference between being and imagination. But imagination cannot spring from nothing: it must be based on people's inner and outer experience. Since individuality and creativity are identical, the creator must always seek the unique, the exceptional, the unusual. Leibniz said that the monads were windowless, but I felt that the monads do have windows. They are al-

lowed to observe each other but are not permitted to imitate. A monad must know exactly when to close its window and pull down the shade.

4. *The lecture version reads: "In my most recent novel, The Slave." This also dates the essay to 1962.*

5. *The lecture version ends with:* Thank you very much for bearing with me and listening to this personal story and personal point of view. If it does not serve any other purpose, it will help, I hope, to clarify the way of thinking of a single writer.

A Personal Concept of Religion

1. *Crossed out:* to Leibniz's Monad of the Monads

2. *Crossed out:* It is true that I believe in God and even in his ability to reveal himself. But I cannot base my belief on actual revelation. Personally, I have never experienced one. Those that are described in holy books have not convinced me of their authenticity.

3. *Crossed out:* It was proven a long time ago that the human mind is too limited to solve this problem, just as it cannot square a circle, or build a perpetual motion machine.

4. *Crossed out:* You might even label him an idol.

5. *Crossed out:* and imagination. I cannot boast with certainty of the existence of my God and his attributes, but I can firmly state that my faith has grown over the years. I still have many questions concerning my God, and I have formulated a whole system of defenses for him and his actions.

6. *Crossed out:* of destroying himself.

7. *Crossed out:* his creative urge often surpasses even time and space.

8. *Crossed out:* is not a commentator

9. *The following paragraph is crossed out:* Like every artist, God is sensitive. Perhaps he wasn't too happy when Spinoza described him as some sort of lifeless machine. He was probably hurt by the twaddle of Feuerbach. However, he may also be vexed by those who profess to speak in his name and who pretend to be privy to all his secrets. The praise is often as petty as the blasphemy. A Creator must possess much patience.

10. *Crossed out:* We cannot, with certainty, serve a God who does not tell us what to do. Human dignity actually demands that such a God be as ignored as he ignores us.

11. *Crossed out:* We have a role to play. We get the power to play it. What is more, we live with the feeling that . . .

12. *Crossed out:* Our role is not one that has already been played. We must first play it—and feel we can play it well or badly. We call this feeling free will or free choice.

13. *Crossed out:* These rules are the best framework within which humanity can function.

14. *Crossed out:* I neither can seek another way, nor do I want to, than the way it is described in these Ten Commandments.

15. *Crossed out:* I accept the Ten Commandments precisely as I do the Principle of Identity, or Nature. It can be said that breathing is an obsession, but at the same time one must keep on breathing.

16. *Crossed out:* . . . as Spinoza believed it to be. In his *Ethics,* Spinoza addresses himself to readers and tells them what they should and should not do. If everything is preordained, then the universe is a finished motion picture, and it makes no sense to employ such words as do and do not. I must—and I want to—believe in free will.

17. *Crossed out:* a strong character, and firm discipline

18. *Crossed out:* For this reason Christians, who feared to tread on a straw cross, could set up an Inquisition; Mohammedans, who observed the fast of the Ramadan and performed all the Muslim good deeds, could burn cities with all their inhabitants; and Jews, who feared a crumb of leavened bread during Passover, could give short weight and false measure.

19. *Crossed out:* Each of these, people must perceive according to their own powers.

20. *Crossed out:* because of this very fact, his every step is fraught with danger. He can, like man, do much good, but he may also do something in his godly experiments that he may regret. What is more, his creation, just like an artist's, is not without consequences.

21. *Crossed out:* If the character of a novel has a black beard in the first chapter, he cannot have a red beard in the second.

22. *Crossed out:* a transition and transformation.

23. Crossed out: "in time and space . . . nor significance and purpose"

24. *The next paragraph begins with:* Thank you very much, ladies and gentlemen, for listening to this personal point of view.

A Story about a Collection of Stories

1. *The original date stated here is 1904 but the date of Singer's birth has long been a point of contention among scholars. Most give it as July 14, 1904, which was the day Singer celebrated in his lifetime. Others use the date more recently proposed by German scholar Stephen Tree, November 21, 1902. Other sources, though, complicate the picture. In Of a World That Is No More (1946), a memoir by his older brother Israel Joshua, Singer is referenced as already being in a cradle during the Jewish year of 5665, which corresponds to 1904–5, and, more importantly, is described as being an infant before Theodor Herzl's death, which occurred on July 3, 1904. And Singer was himself aware of the contradiction, telling Paul Kresh he had two birthdays, one in July, which is the one he uses officially, and one in November, which he said corresponded to the Hebrew month of Heshvan. Dvorah Telushkin also reports his birthday in November, and in* The New York Times, *he tells*

Rabbi William Berkowitz that his "real birthday is in Cheshvan [sic], on a Wednesday during the third week" ("New York Day by Day," Sept. 3, 1984). Stephen Tree suggests he was born in 1902 because in that year the twenty-first of Heshvan falls on November 21 on the Gregorian calendar—but during that time Poland was part of the Russian Empire, which followed the Julian calendar, making the date November 8. Also, Tree's proposed date falls on a Friday, a Sabbath eve, not a Wednesday, as Singer reports. The only other option is the one not yet considered—1903—which corresponds to the Jewish year of 5664. The third Wednesday of Heshvan that year falls on November 11, which conforms with his brother's portrayal of Singer as being an infant in July 1904 and in a cradle in the year 1904–5. It is most plausible, then, that his birthdate is indeed November 11, 1903—give or take about a week.

The Making of a First Book

1. *Crossed out:* Young as I was, I knew the troubles of the sick and the old, and of the disappointed.

To the True Protester

1. *Crossed-out stanza:*

    God of silence, violent man
    Will remain forever the ruling clan
    Might makes right to lord and slave
    It begins from the cradle and ends in the grave
    Yesterday's victim is the oppressor today,
    Hide, protester, and smuggle your way

2. *Crossed-out stanza:*

    As we endure, let's not scold
    Rich or poor, young or old,
    Let's not kill, hurt, mock, or cheat,
    Shed animal's blood, eat its meat
    In our [protest / anguish] let us cry
    Why doest Thou punish the helpless, why?
    While Thine is the wisdom and the might,
    Ours is the right in the darkest night.

BIBLIOGRAPHY

Barzun, Jacques, et al., eds. *Papers on Educational Reform Delivered at the Fourth Annual Meeting of the Open Court Editorial Advisory Board*. La Salle, IL: Open Court, 1973.

Burgin, Richard, and Isaac Bashevis Singer. "Isaac Bashevis Singer's Universe." *The New York Times*, December 3, 1978, sec. SM, pp. 39–52.

———. *Conversations with Isaac Bashevis Singer*. New York: Doubleday, 1985.

Garrett, Leah. "Cynthia Ozick's 'Envy': A Reconsideration." *Studies in American Jewish Literature* 24 (2005): 60–81.

Goran, Lester. *The Bright Streets of Surfside: The Memoir of a Friendship with Isaac Bashevis Singer*. Kent, OH: Kent State University Press, 1994.

Hellerstein, Kathryn. "The Envy of Yiddish: Cynthia Ozick as Translator." *Studies in American Jewish Literature* 31, no. 1 (2012): 24–47.

Hoffman, Warren. "Androgynous Tales: Gender Ambiguity in the Short Stories of Isaac Bashevis Singer." In *The Passing Game: Queering Jewish American Culture*, Syracuse, NY: Syracuse University Press, 2009, pp. 124–45.

Kresh, Paul. *Isaac Bashevis Singer, the Magician of West 86th Street: A Biography*. New York: Dial Press, 1979.

Malin, Irving, ed. *Critical Views of Isaac Bashevis Singer*. New York: New York University Press, 1969.

Miller, David Neal. *Fear of Fiction: Narrative Strategies in the Works of Isaac Bashevis Singer*. Albany: SUNY Press, 1985.

Ozick, Cynthia. "Envy; or, Yiddish in America." In *The Pagan Rabbi and Other Stories*, Syracuse, NY: Syracuse University Press, 1971, pp. 39–100.

Salberg, Jill. "Reimagining Yentl While Revisiting Feminism in the Light of Relational Approaches to Gender and Sex." *Studies in Gender and Sexuality* 13.3 (2012): 1–12.

Schwarz, Jan. *Survivors and Exiles: Yiddish Culture after the Holocaust*. Detroit: Wayne State University Press, 2015.

Singer, Isaac Bashevis. "Verter oder bilder" (Words or Images), *Literarishe Bleter*, Aug. 26, 1927, pp. 663–65.

———. "Tsu der frage vegn dikhtung un politik" (Toward the Question of Poetics and Politics). *Globus* 1.3 (Sept. 1932): 39–49.

———. Lecture on literary method, January 29, 1964. Sound recording, 7″ sound reel, Harry Ransom Center, University of Texas at Austin.

———. *A Friend of Kafka and Other Stories.* New York: FSG, 1970.

———. "What Is God to Do—Discuss His Obit with Every Reader?" *New York Times*, May 18, 1979, sec. A, p. 29.

———. "My Personal Conception of Religion." Lafayette: University of Louisiana, 1980.

———. *Conversations.* Ed. Grace Farrell. Jackson: University Press of Mississippi, 1992.

Stromberg, David. "Rebellion and Creativity: Contextualizing Isaac Bashevis Singer's 'Author's Note' to *The Penitent.*" *In geveb*, June 2016.

———. *Narrative Faith: Dostoevsky, Camus, and Singer.* Newark: University of Delaware Press, 2018.

———. "The Exorcist: The Mystical Storytelling of Isaac Bashevis Singer." *Prooftexts* 38.1 (2020): 94–138.

———. "'Your Papers for a Tourist Visa': A Literary-Biographical Consideration of Isaac Bashevis Singer in Warsaw, 1923–1935." *The European Journal of Jewish Studies* 15.2 (2021): 256–84.

———. "'Don't Be Hopeless, Kid': A Literary-Biographical Consideration of Isaac Bashevis Singer's First Years in New York, 1935–1937." *Studies in American Jewish Literature* 40.2 (2021): 109–39.

Zamir, Israel. *Journey to My Father: Isaac Bashevis Singer.* Trans. Barbara Harshav. New York: Arcade Publishing, 1995.

Below is a list of essays by Singer for further reading, arranged in chronological order of their English-language publication. Though not exhaustive, it includes a number of his more obscure publications.

"Realism and Truth," trans. Adah Auerbach Lapin, *The Reconstructionist* 15 (1962): 5–9.

"What it Takes to be a Jewish Writer," trans. Mirra Ginsburg, *National Jewish Monthly* 78 (1963): 54–56.

"Sholem Aleichem: Spokesman for a People," *The New York Times,* September 20, 1964, sec. 2, p. 1.

"Indecent Language and Sex in Literature," trans. Mirra Ginsburg, *Jewish Heritage* 8 (1965): 51–54.

"Introduction," in I. J. Singer, *Yoshe Kalb* (New York: Harper and Row, 1965), pp. v–x.

"What's in It for Me?" *Harper's*, October 1965, pp. 172–73.

"Once on Second Avenue There Lived a Yiddish Theater (Did it Ever Die?)," *The New York Times*, April 17, 1966, sec. Arts & Leisure, 121.

"Peretz' Dream," *American Judaism* 15, no. 20–21 (1966): 60–61.

"Introduction," in Yitzchok Perlov, *The Adventures of One Yitzchok* (New York: Award Books, 1967), pp. 7–12.

"Knut Hamsun, Artist of Skepticism," in Knut Hamsun, *Hunger*, trans. Robert Bly (New York: Noonday Press, 1967), pp. v–xii.

"Civilizing the Shtetl: Mendele Mocher Sforim on the Fiftieth Anniversary of His Death," *Jewish Chronicle*, December 8, 1967, i–ii.

"The Future of Yiddish and Yiddish Literature," *The Jewish Book Annual XXV* (New York: Jewish Book Council of America, 1967), pp. 70–74.

"The Fable as Literary Form," in *Aesop's Fables*, trans. George Fyler Townsend (New York: International Collector's Library, 1968).

"On Translating My Books," *Papers Delivered at Conference on Translation of Literature* (New York: PEN American Center, 1970).

"Preface," in Lionel S. Reiss, *A World at Twilight: A Portrait of the Jewish Communities of Eastern Europe Before the Holocaust* (New York: Macmillan, 1971).

"Are Children the Ultimate Literary Critics?" in *Top of the News,* Nov. 1972, pp. 32–36. Reprinted in *Stories for Children* (New York: Farrar, Straus and Giroux, 1984), pp. 332–38.

"Art and Folklore," in *Papers on Educational Reform Delivered at the Annual Meeting of the Open Court Editorial Advisory Board* (La Salle, IL: Open Court, 1973), pp. 28–34.

"Jewish Art and Literature," *Encyclopedia Britannica*, 15th edition (1974).

"Yiddish Tradition vs. Jewish Tradition: A Dialogue," with Irving Howe, *Midstream,* June-July 1975, pp. 33–38.

"Banquet Speech" (including "Why I Write in Yiddish" and "Why I Write for Children"), NobelPrize.org, www.nobelprize.org/prizes/literature/1978/singer/speech.

"Foreword," in Dudley Giehl, *Vegetarianism: A Way of Life* (New York: Harper & Row, 1979), p. 11.

"Freedom and Literature," *Parameters: Journal of the US Army War College* 11, no. 1 (1981): 8–12.

"Of Providence, Free Will, and the Future of Learning, *The New York Times*, June 17, 1984, sec. 7, p. 3.

"The Golem is a Myth for Our Time," *The New York Times*, Aug. 12, 1984, p. H1.

Conversations with Isaac Bashevis Singer, with Richard Burgin (New York: Doubleday, 1985).

"Genesis," in *Congregation: Contemporary Writers Read the Jewish Bible* (1987), ed. David Rosenberg (San Diego, New York, and London: Harcourt, Brace, Jovanovich, 1987).

"Foreword," in Ira Moskowitz, *The Drawings and Paintings of Ira Moskowitz* (New York: Landmark Book Co., 1990).

Conversations, ed. Grace Farrell (Jackson: University Press of Mississippi, 1992).

"How Does It Feel to be a Yiddish Writer in America?" *Pakn Treger* 77 (2018).

"Immigration," *Pakn Treger* (2020), https://www.yiddishbookcenter.org/language -literature-culture/pakn-treger/2020-pakn-treger-digital-translation-issue /immigration.

INDEX

abstract art, 50

Acosta, Uriel, 107

Adam, 67, 88, 183

Adler, Alfred, 46, 192

Adler, Celia, 124

Adler, Jacob, 124

Adler, Julius, 124

Adler, Luther, 124

Adler, Stella, 124

advertising, 59

Agudas Yisroel, 106–7

Akdamut, 163, 170

Aleichem, Sholem, 125, 137, 191, 204

Alexander II, Tsar, 123

Alfred A. Knopf, 4

Andreyev, Leonid, 21

animals, 86, 143, 173

Ansky, S., *The Dybbuk*, 126

Anti-Defamation League, 97

antisemitism, 95–97, 104, 115, 191, 192

Aramaic, 116, 130

Aristotle, 44, 54–55, 87

Aryeh de Modena, Rabbi, 85

Asch, Sholem, *God of Vengeance*, 125

Ashkenazi Jews, 114, 116, 132

assimilation: Enlightenment encouragement of, 103, 112, 133–34; literature and, 132, 133, 157; natural inclination toward, 103; Polish Jewry and, 184;

resistance to, 103–5; Yiddish spurned by advocates of, 126; Zionism and, 133–34

Augustine, Saint, 142

authors: anger of, 49; faith of, 48–49, 127, 201; originality of, 45, 51–52, 69; readers' relationship to, 39–40; relationship of, to God, 41, 42, 48–49, 73; relationship of, to money, 59; role of, in writing fiction, 22, 193; talent of, 40–42, 68–69; unique viewpoints of, 55–56

Axenfeld, Israel, *The First Jewish Recruit*, 122

Baal Shem Tov, 79, 80, 142, 147, 190

Balfour Declaration, 113

Balzac, Honoré de, 27, 139

beauty, 40, 42, 50, 72–73, 84, 166, 170

Beliefs and Opinions, 78

Ben-Ami, Jacob, 124

Bergelson, Dovid, 137

Bible: animals in, 86; character and behavior of heroes of, 109–10; Hebrew language of, 28; history of the Jews as portrayed in, 111; interpretations of, 77–78; Kabbalah based on, 87; Sabbatai Zevi and, 188; Singer's experience of, 190; as source of literature, 44

227

Emden, Rabbi Jacob, 85, 190–91

emotions: display of, 65, 67; linguistic expression of, 65–67; particularity of, 66–67; significance of, 64–65; in Spinoza's philosophy, 66, 84, 121, 166

English language: Singer's voice recordings in, 3; translations into, 1–2, 6; writings in, 2

Enlightenment. *See* Jewish Enlightenment

entertainment, as art's purpose, 38–39, 42, 48, 50–52

Esau, 109

eternal questions, 41, 42, 49, 61–62, 79, 156

Ettinger, Shloime, *Serkele*, 122

Euchel, Isaac, *Reb Henoch*, 122

Eve, 67, 182–83

evil, 82, 86–87, 157, 182

excommunication, 104

exile: attitudes toward, 108–11, 116–18, 134, 136; Jewish advances resulting from, 110–11, 180; Jewish community formation in, 102, 107; Jewish experience of, 117–18, 129–30, 180; Kabbalah's conception of, 182; statehood vs., 112–13; as universal experience, 117, 137; Yiddish as language of, 115. *See also* Diaspora

Exodus, book of, 179–80

Eybeschutz, Rabbi Jonathan, 190–91

faith: children as models of, 73; in modern times, 15–16, 117, 143; reformulation of, to include all creatures, 143, 173; Singer's childhood experience of, 77–78, 154–55, 190–92; Singer's personal, 161–64, 168–75, 194n; Singer's questioning of, 78–79; worldly Jews and, 104; writers and, 48–49, 127, 201. *See also* doubt; religion

Farrar, Straus and Giroux (FSG), 4–5

Faulkner, William, 140

Feuerbach, Ludwig, 201

First World War, 156

Flammarion, Camille, 156, 161

Flaubert, Gustave, 44, 62, 158; *Madame Bovary*, 32, 93; *Salammbô*, 21

folklore, 49, 51

Forel, Auguste-Henri, 46

Forverts (*Jewish Daily Forward*; newspaper), 1, 12, 14, 19, 20, 28, 124, 195–97

Frank, Jacob, 85, 190

free choice/will, 82, 128, 173–74, 182

Freud, Sigmund, 27, 46, 47, 69, 88, 93, 180, 192

Fuchs, A. M., 135, 137

Fuchs, Leo, 127

Gandhi, Mohandas, 80, 100, 101, 142

Gemara, 78, 184, 186, 188

Genesis, book of, 72, 183, 190

Genghis Khan, 80

Gersten, Berta, 124

ghettos: confinement to, 102; talents of residents of, 109; Yiddish literature and, 138–40; Yiddish theater and, 120, 126

ghost stories, 19

Giroux, Robert, 5

Gnosticism, 87, 184, 188

God: artists' relationship to, 41, 42, 48–49, 73; children's belief in, 70; and creation, 80–84, 86, 88, 162–64, 166, 168n, 170–75, 181–82; creation of individuals by, 57; criticisms of, 164, 171–72; feminine aspect of, 84, 166, 170, 182, 186; Jews' relationship to, 102; kabbalistic conception of, 79–84, 88, 162–64, 166, 170, 181–83, 185–86, 190; monotheistic conception

Lateiner, Joseph, 123

Lawrence, D. H., *Lady Chatterley's Lover*, 93

Leibniz, Gottfried Wilhelm, 88

Leivick, H., 125

Lenin, Vladimir, 49, 63, 69, 92, 115

Leninism, 73, 130

Lessing, Gotthold Ephraim, 123

Levinsohn, I. B., *The Deceitful World*, 122

Leviticus, book of, 102

liberalism, 73

Libin, Zalmon, 124

Lipshitz, Paula, 151–52

Liptzin, Keni, 124

Literarishe Bleter (journal), 159

literary criticism: formal preoccupations of, 40; misguidedness of, 36, 67; pernicious influence of psychology on, 22, 33, 36; Singer's practice of, 204; Singer's spoofs of, 90–91, 94–98; superfluity of, 22, 33, 38

literature: artificial production of, 32–33; censorship of, 25–31, 25n, 46; character as basis of, 35–37, 46–47, 57; children's, 6, 7, 67–68, 70–73; essence of, 34–40, 47, 54–55; experimentation in, 40; individuality/particularity as basis of, 35–39, 46–47, 57–60; international awareness of, 142; Jewish spirit awaits expression in, 139–40; journalism compared to, 20–24, 33; national nature of, 49–51, 116–17, 133; and nature, 43–45; orientation toward the future as mistake in, 53–54, 62; psychology in relation to, 22, 35, 45–46; purpose of, 32–42, 52; real life compared to, 32; role of information in, 21, 23–24, 35, 47; science compared to, 22–23, 37, 39, 47; sexuality in, 26–28; storytelling

as purpose of, 36, 39, 48, 50, 53–60; subjectivity in, 44–45; teaching not the proper concern of, 37, 39, 45, 48, 53–54; topics of, 59–61. *See also* modern literature

Lodge, Oliver, 156, 161

London, Jack, *The Call of the Wild*, 158

love: in the Bible, 187; in the Kabbalah, 84–85, 165; religious suspicions of, 149; Singer's conception of, 170; Singer's youthful experience of, 149–52; as topic of literature, 59–60, 68, 150; in Yiddish theater, 120

Luria, Rabbi Isaac, 79, 80–81, 87, 161, 162, 165, 181, 184–85

Lux, Lillian, 127

Lysenko, Trofim, 41

magic, 147–51, 179–80, 190. *See also* mysticism

Malthus, Thomas Robert, 89

Manger, Itzik, 135

Mann, Thomas, 11

Markish, Peretz, 125, 159–60

Marx, Karl, 47, 63, 82, 92, 115

Marxism, 73

masses: not the proper concern of literature, 41, 60, 62, 71; political concerns with, 63

Maupassant, Guy de, 21, 27, 38, 62, 158

Mayakovsky, Vladimir, 160

Mearson, Lyon, 4n

Menahem from Vitebsk, Rabbi, 138

Messiah: coming of, 84, 87, 164, 180; Jesus not, 112; pan-Jewishness and, 111; pious Jews and, 107, 109; Sabbatai Zevi and, 186–89; suffering as sign of coming of, 184

Midrash, 83, 87, 108, 162, 188

Midwood, Barton, 204